Journey into Light

The Story of a Woman's Struggle to Heal, Love, and Forgive

by
Gayle Rose Martinez

A.R.E. Press • Virginia Beach • Virginia

A.R.E. Press
Sixty-Eighth & Atlantic Avenue
P.O. Box 656
Virginia Beach, VA 23451-0656

Library of Congress Cataloging-in-Publication Data
Martinez, Gayle Rose, 1951-
Journey into light: the story of a woman's struggle to heal, love,
and forgive/by Gayle Rose Martinez.
p.   cm.
ISBN 0-87604-292-2
1. Martinez, Gayle, 1951-   . 2. Mental healing—United States—
Case studies. 3. Association for Research and Enlightenment—
Biography. I. Title.
RZ406.M27A3   1992
248.8'6'092-dc20
[B]
                                                92-19636
                                                    CIP

Dedication

Thank you to all the people, places, and things that helped guide and support me through this healing journey and to the Master Conductor.

[Preface]

This is my story of coming to find out who I am. A traumatic injury inspired me to survive, and it gave me the means to find myself. A four-year span of my life was a time of great healing—physically, mentally, and spiritually. As I healed, so did my relationships with those I loved most.

My healing journey—especially the years 1979 to 1983 as told in this book—took me to many places I'd never dreamed I'd be in: emergency rooms, operating rooms, an orthopedic clinic, drug rehabilitation counseling centers, courtrooms, and an invaluable year with my young daughters in Virginia Beach, Virginia. All along the way, I was slowly discovering that healing must start as "an inside job." Although it's truly a medical miracle that my body functions in a normal, healthy way today, the source of that outer healing is found deep within me. I had to change inside—going beyond anger, hopelessness, and despair—before my outer healing was possible.

In 1979, at the time of my accident, I had been

married to Steve for six years. When we met in 1966, Steve had already begun his journey with alcohol and needed someone to take care of him. At the age of fourteen, I found caretaking for Steve quite satisfying, even though it required ignoring my own feelings and needs. As I became more empty of "Gayle," I became more proficient at attending to him. One year into our relationship, my own chemical dependency had sur-faced. My story begins in those teen-age years.

[1]

My adrenaline was running high. Steve was coming to pick me up. He was my life. Even though I was only fifteen, I knew this was real love.

As I opened the door to let him in, he slipped me some acid—LSD. I casually walked into the kitchen and got some water to swallow it. Steve never could figure out why I needed water to swallow such a tiny pill, but it had always been like that for me. While I stood at the sink, I could sense his brown eyes on my back burning with impatience. Within minutes we were on the road. I sat close to Steve, feeling his warm, tight body next to mine. He smelled clean and fresh from a recent shower. A feeling stirred in my stomach: a mixture of fear and excitement. It was a feeling I had come to associate with Steve. He looked ready to party in his tight blue jeans and long-sleeved blue denim shirt. His curly, dark brown hair seemed to emphasize his wild spirit. "What's your hurry tonight?" I asked.

Steve flashed me a smile and responded, "I want to get to Max's before I get high."

Max was an older guy who let us hang out in his apartment and get high. "You already took some acid?" I questioned, feeling a familiar struggle with Steve's choices.

"Yea, I took two to make sure I'd have a good time. I wanted you to get started so we'd both be high at the same time." Steve was trying to charm me in his usual way.

I started to feel the familiar rush of the Purple Haze washing over my body. "This is good stuff," I exclaimed.

"Really?" Steve said. "I don't feel anything yet. The guy who sold me this stuff said there was one hit in the bag that's not acid. He said it's something like PEC or PAC—I don't know. But he said it will knock the socks off the lucky person who gets it."

"Who needs anything extra," I thought, "this stuff is great."

As the evening progressed, I wandered into my own space of color and movement. Looking around Max's apartment, I was reassured that this was the best place in the world to get high. It felt safe, and the music was great. Max knew how to melt candles on old wine bottles in that perfect way so that the wax build-up was symmetrical all the way around the bottle. Max was cool. He knew a lot about life. He was almost twenty-six.

Suddenly, I felt nauseous. I went into the bathroom and threw up. There was vomit all over me and the room. I asked Max's girlfriend to come into the bathroom and help clean me up. She wasn't interested in drugs, but drank alcohol. She tried to convince me that there wasn't vomit anywhere that she could see.

"I know just how you feel. When I puke, I feel like it's all over me, too."

She had no idea where I was. I was in the land of rainbows, and now there was a mess all over. I finally went into the living room and noticed that I had come into a new dimension of perception. Max's cigarette was burning backwards. Everything began to melt. Panic started spreading through me as I realized there was nothing to hold onto—nothing solid, no foundation. Max was talking to me. He was telling me to put some round blotches together.

"They're called Diddly Boppers. Try to focus; it will help." He took my hands and put them on the Diddly Boppers. They melted into puddles of paint. "Focus harder, Gayle. You can do it."

It took all my concentration to put two blotches of paint together, but gradually a sense of solidity started to return. "I'm not sure I like this acid, Steve. I think it's too strong for me."

"Don't be such a drag," Steve complained as he returned to his place in time and space.

It was a long night. It was the first time I felt as if I might lose it. Stories of people losing it to acid played with my mind. I felt controlled by the drug. Promises to never do acid again filled my mind. If only I could get through that night. Diddly Boppers became my savior. I was convinced that somebody out there must have known that people on acid would use them to stay more grounded. My brain marveled at the brilliance and forethought of some people.

Finally it came time to head home, and Steve dropped me off. I wondered how I would sleep. My mom was up and approached me as I came in. Stay cool, I thought. I was aware that my eyes were like two deep holes, so I tried not to look at her directly.

"Gayle, it occurred to me tonight that I should tell you something. If you choose to do drugs, don't ever come home stoned. If you do, I'll make you wish you had never, ever taken drugs."

Wow! My mind was exploding. She knows. She's messing with my mind. Get out! Now! "O.K., Mom, I'll remember what you said. I'm going to go to bed now."

Safe in bed, my eyes closed, I was still clearly in rainbow city. "Please, Lord, just help me sleep it off.

I won't do it again."

Morning came in its own time. I was exhausted. Sunday was a good day to laze around. I was O.K., but knew that I had narrowly escaped from entering the land of the permanently insane.

I stayed straight until the next weekend. Then Steve came over, slipped me another hit of acid, and I casually went into the kitchen to get some water to swallow it.

As time went by, the parties lost their appeal to me, and I found myself going to them just to be with Steve. It was a rocky and eventful relationship between two teen-agers. Steve was a wild young man out to experience it all without concern for safety or others. We went to parties, rode motorcycles, made love, and fought constantly. We went our separate ways on several occasions. But I usually sought him out after a period of time. There were other women and other men in our lives, but the passion between us never seemed to dissipate. It was an explosive and eventful process, leaving me angry and bitter. Sometimes it was difficult to separate the love and the hate that came with our encounters.

After five years of dating, I made one final attempt to rid myself of my obsession with Steve. I applied to a college in Washington state—a thousand miles away. When I received an acceptance, Steve realized that I was really leaving, and he asked me to marry him. All my resolve slipped away, as he charmed me into staying in Minnesota. I decided it was hopeless to think of living without him.

We were married on February 26, 1972. Marriage only increased the tension in our relationship. The first year was the worst. We fought about everything, each of us trying to maintain some semblance of power.

Steve was working in the building trade as a crane oiler at this time. His job was to maintain the cranes and transport them to and from job sites. It was a union position, and this year many building trade union contracts were in dispute. Consequently, Steve had fewer opportunities to work. It was a motivating factor in his decision to change careers and become an over-the-road trucker.

Steve was mechanically talented and could learn to operate any kind of vehicle. He was surprised that first week how tired he became after driving a semi for one day. Every muscle in his body ached from wrestling with the big steering wheel and the power of the diesel engine. His body developed the appropriate muscles in his arms and chest, and within a few months he was able to drive cross-country in three days. This work fit Steve's sense of adventure.

When he started driving cross-country on a regular basis, I chose to ride with him for awhile. We found we worked well together. Steve took the lead role, and I accepted that. We agreed to save our recreational use of drugs and alcohol for when we were back in Minnesota, off duty. We put in so many hours working that there was little time to be intoxicated. His new career gave us something else to focus on, and for awhile things were better in our marriage.

In 1974 we purchased our first house, and I gave birth to our daughter Sherri. Steve was proud to be a father. But between his work and his drinking, he didn't actually engage in parenting. Sherri was someone to show off to his friends when she was happy and to give to me when she was not. I became a full-time housewife and mother. My drug and alcohol use declined, mainly because I was rarely included in Steve's social activities. I also found parenting very demanding. The new responsibilities weighed on me, and I became disgruntled. I nagged at Steve about his drinking and complained about his lack of responsibility around the house.

Our time together was limited, and often we found

old issues flaring up again, both of us trying to maintain our personal power and control each other's behavior. I wanted Steve to cut down on his drinking and
show more interest in me, Sherri, and the house. Steve
wanted me to lighten up and give him the freedom he
deserved after putting in long hours in his truck. My
days were planned around his life, and I spent many
hours waiting for him to call or to come home. When
finally we would connect, there was a wall of anger
between us. It was hard to remember that once just
seeing Steve would fill me with euphoric feelings. It felt
as if all the previous passion between us had been
eaten away by unrealized expectations and disappointments.

By 1976, my life was dictated by Steve's mood swings
and erratic behavior. It didn't take much for his anger
to flare. I found myself afraid to talk to him about
anything that might upset him. When he was angry, he
would stomp around, slam doors, and shout accusations at me. Sometimes I would not respond; other
times I reacted with my own rageful accusations. This
collision of anger would instigate a war that would last
for days. In desperation to make my life more manageable, I joined Al-Anon, a program for family members
of chemically dependent people. I thought Al-Anon
would help me find a way to make Steve quit drinking.
I believed that if Steve quit drinking, our problems
would be over. In Al-Anon, I was told that in order to
find any measure of peace, I must put the focus back
on myself.

It was happening again, I thought. At 5:30 I had set
the table, anxiously awaiting Steve's delight at my delicious dinner. The kitchen was filled with the aromas
of his favorite foods, cooked to perfection: juicy roast
beef, gravy, mashed potatoes, corn, and home-made
bread. He had said 5:30; it was now 7:00.

Six months in Al-Anon had taught me not to rescue

my alcoholic spouse. It seemed that the right thing to do was to put the supper away and not reheat it for him when he finally came home. I would stand my ground even if he got angry. So I put the supper away and cleaned up. The tears came and went as I felt the accumulation of my unresolved pain. Television offered little comfort as I half-listened for his car in the driveway. At 10:00 I told myself he wasn't in an accident. I felt like a jerk for still being up. At midnight the tears came again as my misery swept over me.

God, how I hated him—his thoughtlessness, his irresponsible behavior. I half-wished he were dead so the pain would be over and I would finally be free of him.

At 2:00 a.m. I heard his car in the driveway. My mind was racing with all the words that would remain unsaid. I must not let him know I was waiting. He must think I was sleeping and didn't care. I waited for his drunken noises to start as he came through the door. The clock was ticking, my body was rigid and alert. Ten minutes went by, and he didn't come in. I went to the window and looked out.

"He's passed out," I said to myself. "It's got to be below zero out there. I'll be damned if I'm going to go out there and bring him in. He can freeze to death for all I care. That'll teach him to drink."

Fortunately Steve woke up on his own about an hour later and crawled into bed shivering. It took me a long time to see the insanity in my behavior. I had personalized Steve's alcoholic behavior, as if his behavior had something to do with me. I couldn't see that it was his own addiction that was driving his behavior. Foolishly, I was feeling justified in jeopardizing his life, thinking that "freezing to death" would teach him something. I was totally preoccupied with his behavior, letting it dictate my every thought, my every move.

My life was characterized by despair, dread, and

hopelessness. It was difficult to remember if life could be different. The practical demands of motherhood kept me moving through my day. I felt trapped in a stormy sea that offered empty promises and predictable disappointments. The promises that Steve would make to me after a fight ("It won't happen again, I'll drink less") and the promises I made to myself ("I won't wait for him, I won't put up with it anymore"). Stephanie, our second daughter, was born in March of 1978. Her birth was a wonderful experience for me, at a time of intense conflict in our home. I believe she gave me the courage to confront the addiction that plagued Steve and me.

Joining Al-Anon was a constructive move toward finding a solution to my inner pain. After my two years of participation in this program, Steve and I together joined Alcoholics Anonymous in June of 1978, and we began our journey with sobriety. Through this program I learned about the twelve steps of recovery. These steps outlined a simple path to inner discovery and spiritual reconnection.

Another catalyst to this transition in our family was my participation in a study group that focused on prayer and meditation. I had started with this group in 1976, around the same time I connected with Al-Anon. In this group I learned about the power of prayer and how to quiet myself. When I practiced quieting myself, I was forced to acknowledge what was going on inside of me. Through my experience with this study group, I also learned that healing energy could be transferred from one person to another. I understood that the source of this energy was my higher power, which I chose to call "God."

The teachings from Al-Anon and my study group complemented each other. Together they awakened my inner voice, whose cries I could no longer ignore. A conflict was created as I realized how different my life was from what my heart yearned for.

I was determined to change.

All the tools these two programs gave me are crucial to the story of what happened in the next four years— a time of extraordinary difficulty. I used these methods to the fullest extent as I walked through the healing journey that lay ahead. In retrospect, it is clear to me that I was being gently led to the people, places, and things that would help me each step of the way.

[2]

I wanted time alone with Steve to discuss our marriage. Steve wanted to go on a motorcycle trip with his friends. I wanted seclusion and privacy. Steve wanted friends. Steve thought he might become a member of this motorcycle club. I thought our marriage might end, after seven years of struggling together.

I agreed to the motorcycle trip because I believed it would be better than nothing. At least we would be with adults, away from the kids, and we would have some time to discuss our issues. I bought some new bib overalls and a denim-jeans jacket for the trip. Although I believed boots were important for comfort and safety, I was unable to find any I liked. Fatefully, I decided to wear shoes.

My friend Shirley said she would watch the girls for Memorial Day weekend. That was a relief because they would be happy and safe with her. I had met Shirley three years ago. She was a beautiful woman about ten years older than I, and she had a natural affinity for children. During the past three years, she had taught me how to see the goodness and innocence in children, and she had shown me alternative ways to express my anger around them.

Two days before we were to leave, Shirley called and said she couldn't watch our kids. I panicked. The trip was essential. Our marriage was falling apart; we needed some time to decide what we were going to do. Determined to have this time with Steve, I started calling everybody I knew. I pleaded, begged, and promised the moon. I had put off calling Fran because she had six children of her own with which to contend. Desperation finally led me to her. She said yes, although I could hear the reservation in her voice.

Then there was our dog Spike. I had to drive thirty miles to find a kennel that had space available over the holiday weekend. Finally I took the girls to Fran's. I felt a sense of relief as I headed for home in our white pickup. Everything was now in place.

The next morning we got up around 5:30 and packed up the bike. Steve attached our sleeping bags and tent to the back of the bike with bungee cords. The few clothes we brought along were rolled up in our sleeping bags. Steve's bike was a 1948 Harley Davidson that he had found in a friend's barn. When Steve discovered it, there were only 1,200 miles on it, and a mouse was living in one of the gas tanks. He had purchased it about three months ago and had spent his spare time preparing it for trips like this one. The bike was dressed out with the original leather saddle bags, which now contained oil, tools, and a can of beans—what Steve saw as the essentials for bike trips. Steve was very proud of this bike. It represented one of his dreams come true.

Steve looked good in his faded blue jeans and the black leather jacket that had survived his drinking days. I noticed his dark brown, curly hair was starting to get that bushy look and could use a trim. His big brown eyes with those curly eyelashes were flashing with the excitement he felt about this trip. He wore his most charming smile, trying to coax me into joining his enthusiasm. It was his charm that had attracted me to him long ago—his charm and his incredible ability to live life to the fullest.

We gathered at the parents' home of one biker. I could smell the bacon cooking as we rode up. I couldn't understand why someone's parents would cook all this food for a bunch of bikers heading out of town, but I was glad they did. It was chilly, and I welcomed the warm coffee and food. There were about twenty bikes outside, and most of the drivers had riders. I met some of the other women going along. I sensed that many of them knew each other and had been riding together before. They showed me the best way to put my bandana on my head so the wind wouldn't blow it off. Tied in the back of the head with the little point of the triangle tucked under the knot, it was secure. I felt awkward and out of place with all these bikers. My resentment about this trip permeated me, darkening my impressions of those around me.

It had been about six years since I had ridden a bike. I found myself thinking back. All my previous riding involved a lot of amphetamines in my system. Today I had concerns about riding sober. In the past, I had numbed my fears with drugs and alcohol. It was a survival technique I had learned quickly when riding with intoxicated bikers. On those previous trips, caution was related only to spotting police, and safety was connected with close proximity to Steve. In that world, women were treated with little respect, and entertainment took a variety of forms that usually involved young girls and treacherous games. A favorite of Steve's had been playing chicken with cliffs on the north shore of Lake Superior. He and his "bros" would race on their cycles to the edge of a cliff. The winner was the bike that stopped the closest to the edge. Often Steve's drunken smile announced his victory. In this particular arena, I had participated as an observer, fully medicated by my drugs of choice. We sold our motorcycle when Steve started trucking. Looking back, it may have bought us some time.

Bikers committed to sobriety—like the ones on the Memorial Day trip—were a different breed. While I waited for our journey to begin that cold May morning, I wondered what sober bikers did for fun around the campfire. Steve had met these bikers recently at a bike parts sale at the state fairgrounds. They were with Bob, a friend of Steve's from high school. Steve discovered that Bob was sober and riding a bike. Steve hadn't known any sober bikers and was just getting into riding again. Bob introduced him to these friends. They all belonged to a club, called the X-Winos. Steve laughed at the name when he told me about running into Bob. Now we were taking a trip with this club, and Steve was looking forward to becoming a member.

As I reflected on this history, I could feel my resentment building. I was back doing what Steve wanted to do in order to spend time with him. This seemed like the never-ending compromise of my life with him.

We finally headed out after the usual delays involving late arrivals, last-minute bike repairs, and pack adjustments. It was a beautiful day for a ride. As we went down the road, the sound of the bikes around us filled me with excitement, almost against my will. I found riding sober was just fine. Soon I could feel a part of me beginning to mellow.

After a couple of hours, we all stopped at a family restaurant called Perkins to eat lunch. Steve and I sat at a table with two other bikers. First, I was introduced to Grandpa, the leader and founder of the club. He had long hair and a full beard. He was a classic biker except that he didn't smell. His friend's name was Coot, who had a button on his jacket announcing: "Male Chauvinist Pig." I felt my anger stir. I interpreted these words as a boast. There was something else pinned on his jacket—a long skinny object. When I asked Coot about it, he said, "That's an opossum's dink."

Trying to stay relatively polite, I decided to converse with Grandpa. I asked him to tell me about the club. He told me it was for men only, and members had to be dry a year before they could join. I asked Grandpa why women were along on the trip, if they couldn't be members of the club. He said some of the club's trips allowed women to come along, basically to keep the men happy. My brain snapped as I realized that I had misplaced all my hopes for intimate time with Steve. This club didn't even recognize women! Steve expected me to be civil to these men and to enjoy being around the camaraderie that excluded me, based on my gender. Panic seized me, despair clouded my heart. I blurted out, "I don't believe it! I'm sitting at a table with a male chauvinist pig, and I'm spending my weekend with an all men's motorcycle group!" How could I hope to connect with Steve within these parameters? Where would be our opportunity to talk?

Grandpa looked at me, grinned, and said just, "Yup." Steve told me to settle down and eat my lunch. When was I ever going to stop believing that Steve would be straight with me? I fought back the tears as I realized that once again my needs for this weekend were not even in Steve's consciousness. He was here to connect with these bikers, not with me. Whatever enjoyment I had experienced was now gone. I felt like excess baggage.

We camped that night on land owned by one of the bikers. It was a beautiful spot, about thirty miles south of Two Harbors, located in northern Minnesota. Acres of trees covered the land. Only an outhouse and trailer indicated human use. Steve pitched our tent way back in the woods. For the first time, I felt some hope for privacy.

I discovered what sober bikers do on an overnight: fool with their bikes, tell old bike tales, roast marshmallows, and sing along with guitars. This all seemed relatively tolerable to me, and I started to chat with some of the other people on the trip. Old adages were being recalled. Someone quoted his mother: "Always wear clean underwear. You never know when you might get in an accident." We rolled our eyes and laughed. These people were beginning to appear more friendly to me.

I was just settling in when I was told to go to the trailer for a while. The bike club was having a meeting, and only members or prospective members were allowed. That meant Steve was invited. I wasn't. I realized that the other women had found something to do, because they were nowhere to be found. In the trailer I found another uninvited soul, a biker who didn't have the required one-year sobriety. To my delight he also was outraged at being told to go to the trailer. We passed our time finding new ways to describe the injustice we had incurred.

I felt betrayed by Steve—separate. We had drifted so far apart. I wondered if we would ever reconnect or if there had been too many bad years. My mind searched for a time when we had been a team. The year 1973 came to mind, the year when we had started our trucking business together.

[3]

In 1973 I was working in the mailroom of Fairway Foods. It had been a way for me to help out financially while Steve made the transition into the trucking business. I remember my last day there, saying goodbye to Val, my co-worker for the last six months. I had grown fond of her and would miss her. Val was excited about the adventure that lay ahead of me. At the end of the work day, she followed me out to see me off.

When Steve pulled up in his new semi cab, I ran out. My heart was pounding with anticipation and expectancy. Standing at the foot of the cab, I hesitated for a moment, wondering if I would be able to keep my dignity while attempting to reach the door of the cab. Grabbing the bar at the side of the door, I hoisted myself up. To my delight, the height of the cab was not a hindrance at all. From my passenger seat, I could feel the power of the engine and the advantage of the height. I waved good-bye to Val. Her face was full of happiness for me.

Steve had purchased a brand-new 1973 International

truck. We had sold all our belongings and given up our apartment for this new way of life. Our first destination was Detroit.

The truck had a single sleeper in the back. Our dog, Spike, had already made himself comfortable back there. My job was navigator. It felt like a true partnership.

I got sick on that first trip. We were going down the interstate, and I lost it out the window. I forgot that my glasses were on, and they blew off. Consequently, I spent the rest of the trip wearing my prescription sunglasses or being blind. It soon became apparent, as we got lost in Detroit, that my skills as a navigator needed some improvement. And as I helped unload my first semi-trailer, the glamor of trucking started to dim. It was a load of Geno's frozen pizzas. I can't remember how many thousands of boxes of pizza it takes to fill up a semi, but I do remember working in the cold refrigerated van for hours and feeling that we had a long way still to go.

When we got back to Minnesota, we went to Steve's parents' house to clean up. His dad's comments let me know that the trip had taken its toll on me. We had been gone only a week, yet I had lost weight and my face was pale. Constipation and shingles plagued me inside and out. Steve's dad was right, I was a wreck.

Trucking as a life style improved for me when I accepted that my stamina didn't equal Steve's. I learned how to conserve my energy and care for myself. If Steve stayed up all night driving, I slept part of the night. When it was time to unload, I didn't always help. If an opportunity came to go to the bathroom, I grabbed it whether it was timely or not. Even if I had different bodily equipment, I don't think I would have been able to relieve myself in a tin can while driving down the road in a semi. Steve could do this, and he did. Consequently we didn't stop as often as I would have liked. He also could substitute a bag of candy for a meal; I couldn't. He frequently took amphetamines to stay up all night; I did this only occasionally. On the nights that I decided to stay up with Steve and take amphetamines, we had our best talks. Or so it seemed at the time. Actually, looking back at it now, staying up all night with Steve gave me access to time with him. In reality the quality of the talks was poor.

It was a hard time to start in the trucking business. In 1973 the price of diesel fuel was raised from 35 cents a gallon to 50. The independent truckers were striking to draw attention to the problems they were facing, and many of them were starting to go out of business. The only way to make it was either to lower your overhead by getting your truck paid off or to have a fleet of trucks. The quickest way to get your truck paid off was to keep it moving on the road loaded with products. Steve had originally planned to teach me to drive, but in the end he didn't want me driving his truck. I didn't mind; I liked riding and navigating. I also enjoyed being with Steve twenty-four hours a day. Our road trips became routine as we developed our rhythm and our roles.

We saw a lot of America's backyard. I liked discovering the country this way. It seemed that we had an opportunity to see how regular people lived. The men and women we met were often interesting, friendly, and helpful. As truckers, people saw us as hard workers; and, with that, a respect was present when meeting other hard-working individuals. I found farmers to be a unique breed. One time when we were in Iowa, we stopped at a farm to ask for directions to the nearest town. The farmer said he'd never been there, never had a need to. The town was only ten miles down the road.

As my grandma used to say, "We were meeting the salt of the earth." People were usually glad to see us, too, because our truck delivered what they wanted or because we were completing their business transactions by removing what they had sold. Steve was conscientious and after a while built his reputation as a dependable trucker.

When we passed through Las Vegas, we saw trucks whose loads of produce had spoiled. Either they had been sitting for days or their refrigeration units had broken and the drivers had not been attentive. In many cases the drivers had gotten caught up in gambling fever and had lost track of time. It was a sad thing to see, knowing that one spoiled load could cost that trucker his reputation and his business.

Spike, our dog, was like a child to us. There had never been a doubt in our minds that he would come with us when we decided to live on the road. But he had trouble adjusting to trucking. The signs were there from the beginning. Problems had started the very first morning. During the night Spike had wiggled his butt through the steering wheel and had a comfortable bowel movement. Not only was this smelly to wake up to, but Steve's boots were under the steering wheel. He would have shot Spike if he had access to a gun.

That first trip with Spike was stressful for all of us. Once I woke up in the sleeper with piles of his distress surrounding me. I felt as if I would get covered with Spike's essence if I moved. I hollered for Steve to help me, but he couldn't hear me over the noise of the engine. I was finally rescued at the next stop. This incident was a lead-in for many jokes in days to come.

After these unpleasant episodes, I took Spike to the vet and asked him why this was happening. He told me that our dog was not made for trucking, and all that sitting was causing him to become nervous. He expressed it by having untimely bowel movements. The vet suggested we allow Spike to run off his tension whenever we stopped. Spike eventually settled into the traveling routine as we learned to help him find more constructive ways to alleviate his stress.

Life felt manageable when we were working, but

trouble manifested itself whenever we came home to Minnesota. Steve wanted to go bar-hopping in our semi cab. He argued that it was boring to be at one bar all night, and we had no other means of transportation. I was adamant about staying put once we started drinking. We both dug in our heels and wouldn't budge from our positions. This situation was the source of many arguments and much resentment. The resentment was especially mine because ultimately Steve had the keys, so we ended up doing what he wanted.

I lasted only six months riding with Steve on the road, partially due to those awful scenes when we would get home. What's more, in those days there weren't many women on the road trucking. It was a man's world, and women were barely tolerated. I found this wearing. Trucking had become a chore instead of an adventure. The towns started to look the same, and the people didn't offer enough distraction. One thing was becoming uncomfortably clear to me: I was only a visitor in Steve's world of trucking. It was his vision, not mine.

When I found out I was pregnant, I was relieved to have a new direction in life. I decided to quit riding full-time and focus on preparing a home for our child. Steve's child. Life was good again.

[4]

When Steve and I chose to stay sober, he decided to sell his truck. He felt that the life style demanded by trucking would not be conducive to his staying sober. For one thing, it was almost impossible for him to drive all night without amphetamines. He went back to work for the building trade as a crane operator in St. Paul in the summer of 1978. It had been a big transition for him to be home every night the past year, and the Memorial Day bike trip was a nice break for him.

The weather remained warm and sunny for the holiday weekend. The time passed quickly during this three-day trip with the X-Winos. It was good to be outside, away from the demands of parenting. Walking back and forth from our tent site to the trailer, which ended up being the central gathering area, made me aware of my need for exercise. The ache in my suddenly overused muscles and the new color on my arms and face made me feel alive and healthy.

As the holiday weekend began to draw toward a close, we started back on Monday—Memorial Day itself. When we stopped for breakfast, I had a delightful conversation with Marie, one of the ladies in our group. We discovered that we had common interests and decided to connect when we got back home. I felt that I had found a kindred soul among these strangers.

Once we were on the road again, I noted how comfortable my new bib overalls were and thought of how good it would feel to be home again. I leaned back on the sissy bar, a metal bar attached to the back of the motorcycle seat. The sound of the bike's motor was soothing. The day was turning into a hot one, and the heat was making me sleepy. At our next stop I would need to take off some layers of clothes. I decided that I'd probably stay in my marriage because I knew I would never endure a divorce. I still loved Steve under all my anger and pain. My decision was made with more of a sense of resignation than of joy. I was feeling the loss of what life might have been.

I must have fallen asleep with these thoughts in mind. I was awakened by the sound of a loud explosion. The bike was slowing down. I leaned forward and asked Steve if we had a flat tire. He cried out, "We've been hit by a car!"

I looked down and saw my broken thigh bone sticking up from my left leg. I looked straight ahead of me, and a scream came out of me as if it belonged to someone else. I could feel an explosive pressure starting in my toes. I felt it climbing up my left leg. As this pressure passed parts of my leg, those spots felt as if they no longer existed. Instinctively I feared that if the pressure reached my heart, I would die. The thought came to me, This is going to be a lot of work. Then a feeling of fatigue washed through me. It was 3:00 p.m. on May 28, 1979.

Somehow Steve got the bike off the road while hanging onto my leg. Some people carried me to the ground. Someone yelled "Ice!" I could feel the pressure reach my waist, and I sensed my time was short. I started yelling, "God is with me! God is with me!" I could hear Steve near my head. He was crying, "No, no, not you! God, not you!" I had to stop listening to him. I could feel the pressure rising. I told myself not to think about that either. I yelled, "God is with me!"

I heard some voices say, "He sure is."

It helped. I yelled, "God is with me!" Someone again responded, "He sure is."

I became aware of a hot sleeping bag on me. I asked that it be taken off. A man used his belt and put a tourniquet on my leg. I found out later that this man remembered a Boy Scout lesson about tourniquets: use one when there is a danger of loss of life or limb. The blood had been pouring out of the compound fracture in my left femur, and if he had not put that tourniquet on, I would have bled to death. Shortly after he had the tourniquet secure, he became unnerved. He couldn't recall how to maintain it. He vaguely remembered it was supposed to be loosened every so often. My leg was still bleeding, and he was afraid to slacken it. At that moment a passing motorist stopped to help. She was a nurse.

I felt a panic rise up inside me. It felt extremely important to ask Steve for a commitment to stay and take care of the children. After the words came from my mouth, I could see the hurt in his eyes.

He said, "Of course, I'll take care of the children." He wondered why I would doubt that. I asked him again to please stay and look after the children. He said that he would.

The urgency I felt was not relieved by his response. A voice inside me said, "I must stay for the children." Somehow I knew that I was making a major decision.

I became conscious of an ambulance siren, and I realized that it was for me. What a strange and fearful sensation! I heard the attendant say, "Forget the leg. Let's get her to a hospital fast."

I thought, Hey, don't forget my leg! At this

point I knew only that I had broken my thigh bone. I had been lying on the side of the road for half an hour.

We went to a nearby small town. Steve told me that we were at St. Gabriel's, a Catholic hospital in Little Falls. I felt tremendous relief that my injuries were going to be treated soon.

When they transferred me to a table in the emergency room, a condom fell out of my bib overalls and landed on the floor. I was terribly embarrassed that the condom was there for all to see. It would be a long time before I would have the privilege of private life again.

I felt my energy waning. I was not raised Catholic, but I did have a strong belief in prayer. I asked that a nun come to pray for me. When she appeared, her hands felt safe and warm as they were placed under my head. She started to pray, and I noticed that she had bad breath.

We had to wait for the doctor to walk back from his house. He had gone home to eat lunch, but when he got back to the hospital he said he could not deal with such a severe injury. I would have to be taken to Minneapolis. I was concerned that I wasn't going to make it to the city—it was three hours away. He asked me where I wanted to be treated. I said, "General," because it was the only hospital I knew. Stephanie was born there.

My wounds were cleaned and dressed, and I was put into a pressurized bag. Between Little Falls and the Twin Cities, I received two units of blood. No pain medication could be given. They said it was important for me to stay alert.

I could feel my body moving with the motions of the ambulance driving down the road. Part of me was not connected to that body. The piece that still was could barely tolerate the immense throbbing, burning pain that engulfed my body. My nerves felt exposed, raw. My energy was very low, and my mouth was dry. I was not allowed to drink anything because of the high probability I would need surgery once we arrived in Minneapolis.

Time passed slowly. It was harder to tolerate my pain without the supportive encouragement I had received earlier. I was terrified and I felt alone; I wanted someone to comfort me. I could see the back of Steve's head as he stared out the back window, consumed with his own emotional pain. The attendant agreed to talk to me, to help distract me from my pain. It was not her forte and the minutes passed slowly.

It was a three-hour ride, and we were in bumper-to-bumper Memorial Day traffic. The siren didn't help. I felt as if I couldn't go on much longer, but then I heard the attendant calling in our arrival on his radio. It was approximately 7:00 p.m. when we reached the hospital.

[5]

I remember being surrounded by X-ray films in the emergency room. I found out later that they had X-rays of my entire body, looking for injuries beyond my leg. The doctors were amazed that, considering the extensive damage to my leg, no other part of my body had been hurt.

I felt a lot of pain—a hot, sharp, burning sensation—when the doctor shot dye into my leg for the arteriogram. This procedure was needed in order to establish the extent of the vascular damage in the remaining tissue. I was told to remain perfectly still, that the test would determine if they would try to save my leg. The impact of this statement went right over me. All I understood was that it was crucial to be still or something very bad would happen to me.

I tried to be still, but the procedure had to be repeated. The bright lights hurt my eyes, and the constant pain felt unbearable. Waves of exhaustion washed over me. I felt pins being stuck into the bottom of my foot. The doctors were happy I could feel the pins. I was overwhelmed that they were adding to my pain. I desperately felt I should tell them I was chemically dependent.

I could feel myself dying, the last of my energy leaking out of my body. I whispered, "I can't take anymore." I don't know if I was heard.

Then the doctor said, "We'd better get her into surgery, stat." It had been five hours since my accident, and I had remained conscious the entire time.

As they wheeled me down the hall, my sister-in-law Linda kissed me. I was surprised to see her since we were not close. Her kiss felt like life to me. I asked her how I looked. She said that they had accidently given me some bad blood in Little Falls, and it caused a rash around my eyes. Other than that I looked fine.

I was told later that, at the time I received this blood, one of the bikers had been on the phone adding my name to a prayer chain. I felt that those prayers protected my body from this "bad blood" and lessened my reaction to it.

I asked Linda why she was here. She said my dad was here, too. I felt worried about that. He wouldn't like being here, and he wouldn't have come unless someone told him my condition was serious. I learned later that Steve had called them both as soon as we reached Minneapolis. They both lived in town.

Only much later did I myself learn how serious my situation was. Both the oncoming car and our motorcycle had been going 65 miles per hour. The car had hit me just below my knee, and the impact on my leg had caused it to explode. The result was a compound fracture of my femur. That was the bone I saw while I was on the bike. Three inches of my leg below my knee were now gone. The bottom of my leg was attached to the rest of my leg by only a flap of skin two inches in diameter as well as by the innermost part of the muscle that forms the calf, the gastrocnemius. This muscle is divided into three parts, and it was the inner part that was still attached. My sciatic nerve, which runs through the entire leg, must have clung to this muscle and had survived the injury. If my leg were to function again, I would have to grow back three inches of muscle, skin, bone, tissue, veins, arteries, and nerves.

In the surgery a Schneider nail—a long metal rod about the length of the bone—was inserted into my femur to stabilize the bone and allow it to heal. The wound below my knee was cleaned and irrigated. Then two metal plates were put on either side of my leg to hold the two pieces together.

I awoke in the recovery room feeling as if I were in heaven. I was lying under hot blankets, and someone was watching over me. My body seemed calmer and the pain was manageable. I still did not understand the seriousness of my injury. At this time, my mind could comprehend only that I had broken my leg. I was moved to the Intensive Care Unit (I.C.U.) and a nurse offered me some ginger ale. This confirmed my sense that I was in heaven because no one on earth ever offered me ginger ale to drink, and it was the only soda I really liked.

When Steve came in, he looked terribly concerned. His face was drawn and pale. Our visit was brief. I told him not to worry, everything was O.K. now. He gave me a sympathetic look and said gently, "Yea, everything is O.K. now." I asked him why he was so concerned; it was just a broken leg, and I felt fine now. I told him I would be home soon. He put his hand on my arm and tried to muster up a convincing smile. His charm failed him. He told me he had been instructed not to stay long and that he would come back later. As he walked away, he appeared to have the weight of the world on his shoulders. My heart went out to him.

I asked someone how long I would be in the hospital, and I was told at least six weeks. I responded, "No way! I could never be away from home that long." I was needed at home.

Because I appeared alert and lively, the doctors allowed me to leave I.C.U. within a few hours after I arrived there and be taken to a regular room. I was probably in either a state of shock or grace those first few days; that was why I didn't feel a tremendous amount of pain and was so lively. It was providential that I was taken out of I.C.U. because soon after I was removed, an infection broke out in the unit. Actually, the amount of attention I required was more than a regular floor nurse could handle, but once it was known that the infection was flourishing in I.C.U., I could not be returned. Not only was I protected from that danger, I was also put into a much friendlier environment where visitors could freely come and go.

My new room was full of machinery. I had an I.V. in each arm and one in my chest. My leg was covered in bandages with hoses running through them. Nurses were in my room constantly checking my I.V.s. I was fairly comfortable for the next two days. I was also very busy. On both May 29 and 30, I was taken to surgery to have my wounds cleaned. During that second day's surgery, the medial part of the gastrocnemius muscle was slit and wrapped around my leg to form the base for a future skin graft. In addition, a bone graft was performed using cells from my left hip to encourage bone growth in my leg. On May 31 I was taken into surgery to stop an arterial bleeder. One of the arteries in my leg was bleeding, and it needed to be tied off surgically to stop the bleeding.

Despite these constant procedures, my spirits remained high. When I looked down on my leg, all I could see was a wad of bandages with my toes sticking out. The doctors were excited and impressed that I could wiggle my toes, although it took an incredible amount of energy to do it.

The bikers from the trip came to visit constantly. It was odd to see them there because I didn't feel as if I knew them very well. The accident had left an impression on them. Bug, one of the bikers who had been riding in front of us, told me he saw in his rear-view mirror my shoe fly off. At the time he thought it was my foot. He came with his girlfriend Lori and expressed his relief that I was doing so well. Tim, the man who shared my anger in the trailer house at being excluded from the bikers' meeting, came often to visit. He said Grandpa told him to come because it would be good for his sobriety. We didn't chat much. He sat on the floor, leaning against the wall, and gave me news about the outside world. Dawn, one of the women who had chatted with me while I waited for the ambulance, came and sat quietly by my side. She was a beautiful blonde woman, and I was grateful for her peaceful visits that didn't demand anything from me. At the same time it was strange to have her come because I didn't really know her.

For the first several days I was in the hospital, the bikers organized a continuous vigil of support for Steve. He was in constant contact either by phone or in person with his "bros"—his spiritual brothers.

After a few days in the hospital, things began to change for me. The state of grace seemed to end. The impact of the injuries consumed my body, which felt as if it had collapsed. I experienced a feeling of incredible heat, and images of a jungle came into my head. I felt as if my body were sinking into a jungle floor—hot and wet—and I was unable to move out of it. I was suffering from a high fever.

I now believe that at that time I was making another major decision to endure and fight it out. During this struggle Doctor Lindqueist stayed with me all night. He was tall, young, with Scandinavian features, and was fulfilling a three-month internship in orthopedics. I believed he was an angel sent to watch over me. He was a Christian, and he prayed for me during that difficult night, as he continued to do while I was under his care.

When I revived from the high fever, my neck was stiff from lying in one position so long. I had to ask for help to start moving it again. But that wasn't my only problem. The nurses instructed me to blow into a blue tube every so often to keep my lungs working. This was standard procedure for all surgical patients. It required as much effort as would be needed to blow into a whistle. My body was so weak that I found this to be a hard challenge. Adding to my discouragement, I realized at this point that I had lost the ability to wiggle my toes.

Morphine was administered around the clock to help me manage pain. My arms felt thick and numb from receiving those shots. When the needle went in, it felt as if it were hitting leather. The incredible pain from my leg made me hypersensitive to any movement. Even someone walking into the room was intolerable. It took all my energy to cope with such a disturbance. I found chatting with visitors to be exhausting, but people seemed to understand and didn't push me to talk much. My room was full of flowers and cards, but I had no awareness of who had sent them. My vital signs were taken constantly, and blood was drawn daily. What they did with all that blood is still a mystery to me.

Regularly my bandages were changed and my wound cleaned. At first I was taken into surgery and put under anesthesia each time; but then one morning, my doctor announced that they were going to start doing this routine in my room with no anesthesia. He told me that two-thirds of the skin below my knee was gone and that I would find the procedure uncomfortable. Experience had taught me that "uncomfortable" was a clue that this was going to hurt. He said it was important for me to relax my leg to the best of my ability. I was then introduced to Doctor Andrews. Linda had remarked that he looked like Mick Jagger. Immediately I didn't like Doctor Andrews because he didn't seem to care about me as a person, as did Doctor Lindqueist.

One fact became clear to me later: my personal preference about doctors and their bedside manners wasn't a good measure of their ability to help me. I was told at a later date about the extraordinary work of Doctor Andrews and Doctor Rothmen (another one I felt who didn't care about me as a person). Their incredible egos and radical approaches kept me from having my leg amputated the first few weeks. They were the physicians in the emergency room the night I arrived. Only young, ambitious surgeons would have even attempted to save such a mangled leg.

Dr. Lindqueist told me it would be better if I didn't look at my leg while they changed the dressing. So I closed my eyes and concentrated on relaxing, asking for God's help and paying attention to my breathing. But I constantly made descriptive comments to the doctors, describing in detail the incredible pain I was feeling. "It feels like my skin is being ripped off in thin strips starting at the top of my leg." Somehow it was helpful to me to let them know what tortures I was experiencing.

I quickly grew to dread these daily procedures. Every morning I had to psych myself up to contend with them. One morning I woke up to find that my energy was so low that I couldn't prepare for my bandage change. Doctor Lindqueist came in and knew right away I wasn't doing well. He told me they would have to start the procedure even if I wasn't ready. It had to be done. As he started preparing the environment for the sterile procedure, my Unity church minister Don Clark walked in. He was in his late forties, of average height, with kind dark eyes. This was his first visit, and it came as a surprise to me. My attendance at church was irregular at best. My doctor, bless his soul, said, "Gayle, you need him more than you need me right now," and left us alone. Don prayed for me and offered a healing of my spirit. He placed one hand on my forehead, and then he lifted his other hand facing upward toward the ceiling. As he prayed aloud, asking the Lord to give me the strength and courage to continue the path I had chosen, I felt calm come over me. It was as if a heavy curtain were lifted, and my situation seemed lighter, more manageable. My spirit was energized, and I was renewed with a positive attitude. When my doctor returned, I was totally prepared for the procedure.

[6]

I had a hard time managing the pain. My mind said, "Rise above it," but I didn't know how. I had asked Steve not to bring Stephanie to visit. She was only a year old, and the thought of all her energy and movements around me seemed unbearable at this point. However, he did bring Sherri to visit. She walked in holding her dad's hand, her big blue eyes were as big as saucers. Sherri looked so little and scared next to her father. Surrounded by all my machinery, she held her little four-year-old body tight. Finally she managed to smile and said, "Hi, Mommy. I'm sorry you hurt your leg."

Just seeing her broke down the wall I had built—the self-protective barrier I had needed in order to cope with missing my children. I wanted to hold her tight and tell her it was going to be all right. I tried to cover my pain and allowed myself to tell her only that I was glad she could come to visit me. Then I asked her to help her daddy with Stephanie. At that moment I wished I hadn't told Steve not to bring Stephanie. My heart pain was worse than any physical pain her visit may have caused. After they left, I worried how they would manage. Steve didn't even know how to change a diaper. It was so overwhelming for me to think about that that I had to push it out of my mind.

I felt as if I might go mad with the pain in my body, the constant battle of being in the hospital, and the pain in my heart from being separated from my family. I needed some answers and some new tools in order to work with this devastating life experience.

One night I had a dream in which I asked to talk to God. I was angry and I wanted some answers. I found myself sitting on a tree branch, conversing with an owl whom I knew to be God. I told God that I could see some value in this opportunity, but why did I have all this pain?

He replied, "There is a tremendous amount of anger and bitterness within you. This is one way of releasing it." I was then given an affirmation to help me heal. It went:

> Thank you, leg, for all the hard work you are doing to heal. Thank you, blood, for flowing strongly through my leg. Thank you, tissues, for your continuous growth of healthy new cells. Thank you, nerves, bones, and muscles, for your continuous strength and renewing. God bless this leg.

When I woke up, I asked a night nurse to write down the affirmation on a piece of cardboard and attach it to the top of the bed frame. She wasn't too busy and thought it was harmless. So she took the bottom of a box of roses, wrote the affirmation on it, and stuck it on the pole that went across the top of my bed.

I lay in bed looking at the affirmation and felt a sense of renewed hope even though the anger and bitterness in my heart ran deep. I knew it was eating away at my soul, and I believed that this could be an opportunity to release and heal these feelings. In my mind I imagined the Memorial Day accident. I could see that the car had selected me from all the bikers on the road that day. It had hit just my leg, injuring no other part of me, and it had not even scratched Steve. At this moment there was no doubt in my mind: this accident was a result of divine intervention. Immediately my dream of the owl came back to me. God was actively promoting the healing of my leg. I could feel my spirit soar as I contemplated the implications of all this. Right then, I asked God for a *total healing* within ten years, leaving only a few scars to remind me of where I had come from. In return I would be His advocate here on earth and tell of this miraculous healing. I would show people His work. I would also devote my life to His service.

The next day I asked the nurses to let me talk to the patient whom they thought was best handling pain. I suspected the visit would allow me to get some help in managing my own pain. They brought in a lady in a wheelchair whose middle finger had been injured by a commercial spray gun. Paint had been injected into her fingernail at close range. Her finger was to be amputated soon. She was in incredible pain, yet she was calm. Her visit was short but her example was powerful. I appreciated her expending energy to come to my room. The only advice she offered was to occupy my mind with things other than my pain. I found that having the TV constantly on helped. I watched shows that were light-hearted and not too loud. I learned that the television evangelist Robert Schuller had a daughter who was struggling with a leg injury similar to mine. Listening to his prayers and talks about her recovery helped me.

People were a constant source of strength. The bikers from the trip visited often. They told of the community support for me. A dance had been organized to raise money, and a Mass had been said for me. Many people and groups from different faiths were praying for me. Another motorcycle club of sober bikers also raised money for me. It was a new experience to have all this attention, and I felt uncomfortable receiving it. When the bike club came to my hospital room and presented me with the $200 they had raised, I didn't know how to react. A part of me wanted to say, "You must have the wrong person." I could tell that they were sincere and deserved some words to take with them, but I was practically speechless. It felt good to have so many people thinking positive thoughts about me, but I felt inadequate responding to it.

I also received strength from a stained-glass window on a church that I could see from my room. At night it was lighted and served as a constant reminder that I was being watched over.

One night I had a dream about a woman named Fran, who had become my friend through the prayer and meditation study group. In the dream I was trying to contact a healer. I couldn't reach her, so I tried calling Fran on what seemed like a telephone. I managed to get through, and I asked her if she would contact a healer for me. I felt as if I were in Grand Central Station. I was surrounded by voices and noises—chaotic communications among people.

I was suddenly awakened from the dream by the phone ringing in my room. It was Fran. She said she had just awakened in the middle of the night with worries about me. She just had to call. We laughed at our ability to connect telepathically. In my heart I was glad that Fran was able to hear my request, and I felt once again supported at a deeper level.

Receiving a phone call at this point in my recovery was not a simple matter. I had I.V.s in both my arms and could not use the phone without assistance. If someone called my room directly, the phone had to be answered by someone else and placed by my ear. I asked Fran to call Beth Zemman, a Reiki practitioner, and to ask her to start sending me an absentee healing—healing directed to someone not physically present with the healer. I didn't know Beth personally, but I had heard of her work through mutual friends. Beth started sending me absentee healing as soon as she spoke with Fran. Later, when it was easier for me to answer my phone, Beth would call me before she sent a healing. On those occasions, I told the nurse that I was about to receive a healing and it would take about thirty minutes. I simply asked the nurse to put a "do not disturb" sign on my door. After that time had passed, she would peek in to see if the healer had gone. This was my private joke. I never told any of the nurses that it was an absentee healing.

Often these healings allowed me to have a restful sleep. This was invaluable because sleeping was difficult. My nights consisted of a series of light naps. I woke up at the slightest movement near me. My vital signs were taken throughout the night, and often other patients made noises. The orthopedic ward was full of people in pain, and at night you could sometimes hear them yell out.

I was given morphine continuously for about the first two weeks. It made me feel sluggish, and I experienced hallucinations. I saw people in my room who weren't really there. Of course, I didn't want anyone to know I was hallucinating, but I wasn't sure when it was happening. So I asked questions whose answers would let me know if what I saw was real. For example, I said to one nurse, "Isn't it after visiting hours now?" When she didn't acknowledge that there was a man standing in the corner of my room after visiting hours, I assumed this was an hallucination.

Sometimes these hallucinations were horrifying. Needless to say, I found morphine to be an unpleasant drug. It didn't really diminish the pain. Instead it made me stop caring about it. Certainly, anything that kept me from focusing on the pain was helpful. But the drug had such a heavy effect on me that I lost my incentive to occupy my time with anything other than watching TV.

Projects also helped me to manage my pain. I had many of them: books to read, crossword puzzles to work on, and various handcrafts to do—after I had the use of my hands. I remember the surge of freedom I felt when they removed the I.V. from one arm. I could answer my phone, feed myself, and actively participate in bed pan use. I was so grateful.

A friend had someone make a special tape for me— one that I could use to help me go to sleep. It was similar to a reverie, with positive statements that reinforced my ability to cope and help me to let go of the pain. I never heard this tape all the way through because it would put me to sleep. And ironically, after I had no more use for it, the tape broke.

With so much time to practice, I eventually became very good at detaching from a painful part of my body. This was a mental exercise, somewhat like blocking out uncomfortable thoughts and memories. As weeks went by, I learned to detach from a painful body part for hours at a time. It worked as long as no one drew my attention back to that part of my body. When I was in this detached state, I believe I also shut down alarm systems my body normally used to draw attention to a problem area. For instance, if I developed a bed sore from lying in one position too long, that area would start to hurt. With my mental exercise, I could disconnect from that part of my body and not feel the pain. But this "disconnecting" made me realize just how needy certain wounded parts of my body really were. Consequently, I was especially grateful for everyone's prayers. I felt they helped protect those parts of myself that pain had forced me to disconnect from.

I learned another approach to deal with pain—almost the mirror opposite of the disconnecting technique. It was to confront my pain head on. I liked this method because it was similar to my approach toward almost all problems in life. It also gave me a sense of power over a situation, a sense of being in control.

Pain initially is a short message sent by the brain to indicate an injury. It's an automatic message not connected to thought. But in some cases, prolonged pain is caused by thoughts. I found that sometimes by letting the feeling pass through me, acknowledging it, and going with its intensity, the pain would leave after a short time. This was difficult for me to do. It required that I be relaxed and centered, and it took a great deal of energy and concentration. It was helpful to believe that the pain would be there for only a short period.

I had already had experience working with pain this way: labor and delivery of my girls. When Sherri was born, I didn't work with my birthing pains. I was tense, angry at the pain, and wanted it to go away. This response only intensified my distress, and I felt victimized by the contractions. But when Stephanie came along, I had decided to be better prepared for the birth. I had a wonderful midwife who helped me stay focused. I worked with the contractions, and I found the experience to be much more manageable.

Being in an orthopedics ward, I saw many examples of people dealing with far worse pain than mine. This helped me to keep my life in perspective and stay away from constant pity parties.

There seemed to be no easy answer to my pain. Trying to cope was like reaching into a bag of tricks— an array of approaches I constantly turned to when in need. I was forced to try different methods at different times, depending on my state of mind. Often I was directed intuitively toward a particular technique.

On one occasion when I had returned from a surgery full of pain, it occurred to me that singing would be a good distraction. The only songs for which I could remember words were nursery rhymes, such as

"Twinkle, Twinkle, Little Star." Perhaps, from singing them repeatedly to my children the words had stuck with me. I found singing to be a very pleasant distraction. After a while I noticed a silly smile on the nurses who came into my room. I asked what was so funny. One nurse told me that I had entertained the ward all afternoon with my tunes. In my medicated state, I must have lost track of time.

[7]

I was scheduled to have a skin graft on June 7, 1979. There had been a constant risk of infection in the open part of my leg due to the loss of skin. The doctors were concerned about a possible infection brewing in my system because I had been fighting a high fever for the past three days. This was the second time it had spiked since my admission. They had been watching me closely and were anxious to get my leg covered with some skin. Infection would be a reason for immediate amputation.

Amputation was a constant threat in my mind and a motivation to do whatever I had to do to heal. The night before this skin-graft surgery, I felt sick to my stomach. I told the night nurse I thought I might throw up. She seemed excited and told me not to do that, that my leg was too unstable to take any jarring. I was given some medicine to alleviate the nausea.

In the morning the doctors came to take me to surgery. I asked them if they knew I had been sick during the night. They didn't know and quickly read my chart.

I was immediately examined, and Doctor Lindqueist ordered a sonogram of my gall bladder. He sent a nurse with me—one who knew me well—so I would be watched over closely. An unfamiliar doctor tried to examine me, but I pleaded with him not to touch me on my right side. Perhaps the nurse intervened on my behalf at this point—I don't remember—but by the grace of God the doctor didn't pursue his examination. All I can recall is being in a great deal of pain. The next thing I remember is waking up in the recovery room. My gangrenous gall bladder had been removed. I learned that gallstones had plugged the drainage tube from my gall bladder, causing it to become swollen with gangrene. It would have soon burst, so the doctors had acted quickly.

Now I felt that God was taking my bargain seriously and had started my total healing process. The recovery time necessary from this surgery delayed my skin grafting another week. Doctors inserted a tube down my throat for a while, and I wasn't allowed to eat for about five days. I had a drainage tube in my side just below the incision from my gall bladder surgery. The surgeon who had removed my gall bladder came and tugged on it. He explained to me that this tube was inserted to allow excess fluids to be drawn off. He pulled it out a little bit each day to keep it from adhering to my body and to keep it from plugging up.

General was not only a county hospital; it was also a teaching hospital for medical students, and because of this I was given new doctors every three months. Dr. Gustillo, the head physician who ran the orthopedic department, was the only doctor I had consistently, and he was renowned for his talent. Otherwise, the rotations came in threes: resident, intern, and medical student. They all had to examine me and ask independently the same questions. I felt violated by all these doctors looking at my body, all sticking me with needles and doing painful procedures.

When my gall bladder doctor was added to the list, I lost it. He came one day to tug at my drainage tube. When he carefully lifted my covers to expose my right side where the drainage tube was located, I pulled off my covers and yelled, "What difference does it make? I don't feel like it matters anymore if I'm covered." The doctor seemed embarrassed at my gesture and covered me quickly. He said, "It still makes a difference to me."

That helped me a lot. I felt he saw me as a person instead of an interesting case. At this moment I needed someone to care about my dignity.

It was painful to move my torso after this gall bladder surgery. It hurt to cough or laugh. I had been instructed to cough and blow into a blue tube to strengthen my lungs and clear any congestion created during anesthesia. To ease the pain of coughing, I held a pillow to my side tightly when I coughed. It helped, but I was glad when a week had passed and the pain diminished.

On June 11 I was finally allowed to eat and was informed I could order *anything* I wanted. I craved tuna fish casserole. The nurses gave me a hard time about ordering such a common dish when I had so many options. It was a great day. I felt alive again. Just as my meal was delivered, my aunt arrived with my cousin Lucy for a visit. This aunt was my dad's sister, Dorothy. My aunt lived in town, but my cousin lived in Alaska. Luckily, I had to eat only a few bites to let the doctors know my digestive system was working O.K. I was so happy to see her and my cousin that I found it hard to eat.

I hadn't seen Dorothy or Lucy in years. Their visit brought back warm memories of my childhood. Our families shared Thanksgiving and Christmas together during my childhood. She was always very kind to me. It meant a lot to me that these two had come. They brought a gift: a pink terry cloth gown to replace the hospital gowns I had been wearing. It became a favorite of mine.

There were signs my physical condition was improving slightly. On June 12 I had my first full day without a fever. But unfortunately after my gall bladder surgery, I developed a yeast infection in my mouth, vagina, and open wounds. My room smelled like a bakery. The problem stemmed from the massive amounts of antibiotics I was being given. Yeast infections plagued me whenever I was given antibiotics. I developed a rash on my buttocks from sweating and lying on my back constantly. The common perineal nerve in my left foot stopped functioning, leaving me unable to hold my foot up. This condition is called "foot drop," and to this day I still am unable to pick up my left foot. I eventually adapted to this condition and found it didn't interfere with my ability to walk.

So many issues in need of healing surfaced during this time. The removal of my gall bladder seemed to be just the beginning of a long process. My pain forced me to focus on myself and take charge of the few pieces of my life I still was able to manage. My body and spirit were facing an onslaught of antibiotics, intrusive examinations, and immobility. I needed to find more tools to help me survive. But with the breaking of my fever on June 12, I surrendered to something Higher— I had faced this ordeal and had broken through some of the anger and bitterness in my heart.

[8]

Shortly after Steve returned to the building trade he was employed by a company that owned tower cranes. The company was willing to teach him how to operate this machinery. It was a great opportunity for Steve. Unfortunately, it didn't survive the demands of single-parenting and caring for an injured wife. Every time I had a surgery, the doctors would call him to report on the results. He had to stop and climb down the crane (which was typically ten or more stories high), talk to the doctors, then climb back up. This halted all construction for half an hour. Eventually he requested that the doctors call only if something was wrong. But the work days missed due to sick kids, unavailable day-care, and sheer exhaustion caused him to lose this position.

Before my accident, Steve had been an absent parent. When he was an over-the-road trucker, he was home about three days out of every two or three weeks. Then, when he returned to construction, he worked long hours and rarely spent time with the children. By that time I was so used to running everything myself, I wouldn't let him do anything. Not only did I believe I was the better parent, I assumed Steve was not capable of doing anything domestic.

Consequently, Steve was thrown into full-time parenting without much experience. The chaos at home became evident quickly. My brother took the girls to his home in Eveleth, in northern Minnesota, for the first week of my hospitalization, allowing Steve time to find day-care. A few days after the girls returned home, Steve expressed a concern to me: Stephanie wasn't drinking anything. I was amazed that he didn't realize that she still needed a bottle. He also couldn't find the dog, and I couldn't remember the name of the boarding kennel where I had left him. Two weeks later Spike was located.

Sherri at the age of four was more like a mature child of eight. Her smooth face was surrounded by thick brown hair that had a natural bend at the ends. She liked to wear her hair short with barrettes on the sides. I had always counted on Sherri's help around the house because she seemed to have been born with a sense of responsibility. Her nature was similar to her father's: social and charming, with an eye for aesthetics. At the age of two she picked color-coordinated clothes from her drawers to wear each day, with her first choice always being a dress. Like her dad, Sherri also was a hard worker. She was able to clean her room at the age of three better than I would.

During my hospitalization Sherri and Steve became partners. They formed a relationship that had never before had time to form. Years later Sherri still remembers this as a time of sadness, but she also recalls with joy this special time with her father. She remembers being able to stay up late with him and watch TV, as well as joining him for rides on his motorcycle. She liked the attention she received for helping her dad. She showed Steve where things were in the house and how to change Stephanie's diapers. She became his right-hand woman. In short: they had a chance to bond.

Steve's long work hours frequently meant later supper hours. The younger, Stephanie, often fell asleep in her food before he could get the entire meal on the table. Her personality was very different from Sherri's. She was like a fairy, flying around somewhere in the ethers, with only one toe connected to earth. Everything was a game, and each game lasted only moments. She had blonde curly hair and brown eyes with beautiful, full lashes. Steve said that in my absence she sometimes exclaimed, "Mommy?" when they passed other women. Taking her to a fast-food restaurant was futile because she was so distracted by the people around her that she never ate her food. Stephanie was always getting dirty and could care less about clothes.

When his time and energy allowed it, Steve bundled up the girls and came to visit me—although at first he followed my request that he bring only Sherri. But basically he was in survival mode himself and couldn't be there much for me. When they came to visit, I could see that Steve had made sure the girls looked tidy. But he looked exhausted, and I couldn't imagine how he was coping. Sherri usually sat on my bed, and I told her the news about my healing process. She would tell me about day-care, but I never heard about what went on at home.

Sometimes I cried from frustration at not being able to mother my children; other times I was able to trust that somehow they would survive. My respect for Steve was growing as I watched him carve out this new life for himself. At the same time my heart was aching because we had never been so distant, each engaged in our own fight for survival.

Steve decided to sue the person who had hit me. I was told that it had been a hit-and-run accident. The bikers went after the car and brought it back to the scene. Someone thought to take pictures of the blood and damage to the car, which was helpful because right to the end the driver denied hitting me. The driver was a sixteen-year-old, who was accompanied by his mother. He was going north and, as he came out of a curve in the road, he spotted the bikers heading south. As we passed by him, he turned to watch us, but in so doing he also turned the steering wheel and crossed over the center line by four feet. He hit my leg, pulled his car back straight, and kept going. The initial charge was reckless driving and crossing over the center line. This was later reduced to careless driving.

I told Steve that I did not want to sue the boy. I felt it was an accident, and his parents should not be held responsible for their son's mistake. Steve was furious about what had happened to our lives. He wanted retribution. His lawyer convinced him there was a great deal of money to be had by suing the young driver and his family.

[9]

The time finally came for me to have my skin graft. Many prayers were said for its success. Normally about fifty percent of a skin graft does not adhere. But in my case it was crucial that more than half of this graft adhere in order to decrease the risk of infection.

Two patches of donor skin were removed from my right thigh. One patch was three-by-eight inches and the other was four-by-eight. The skin was put into a machine that punched tiny holes into it. This increased the size of the donor skin by allowing it to stretch more. It was then very tediously sewn onto my left leg.

Because there was such a large area missing from my leg, the surgeons had previously split the remaining piece of my gastrocnemius muscle and wrapped it around my leg to form a base for the donor skin to cover. This reconstructive surgery was forming my new leg. The muscle unfortunately did not reach all around my leg, leaving a space about one-and-one-half inches square that was open to heal on its own. I called this opening my hole. It offered me an opportunity to look inside my leg. At first, all I could see was emptiness, dark and hollow. But as time went by, I began to see pink, healthy tissue growing and white bone chips being expelled by my body.

After the skin-graft surgery, the doctors bandaged the donor sites on my right thigh. Several days later, when they began to remove those bandages, the strips of cloth stuck slightly to the remaining inner layers of raw skin. The pain of those bandages being removed was excruciating. They had told me it wouldn't hurt, so I was totally unprepared for what happened. Experiencing painful procedures with no previous preparation deteriorated my trust level, increased my fear, and caused me to suffer psychologically. This particular experience was magnified when the doctors discounted what happened with statements like, "Now that wasn't so bad, was it?" or "I have seen bandages stuck worse than these. You were lucky."

Finally the bandages were removed from my left leg to determine the success of surgery. I was very anxious. I had been told to lie still for many days because movement could hinder the success of the skin graft. I had lain very still for quite a few days awaiting the outcome. Beth had sent many healings to my leg during these days.

I received wonderful news! Seventy-five percent of the donor skin had adhered! This remarkable result meant that I didn't have to repeat the surgery. Success also meant no more morning bandage changes.

It was now that the doctors first suggested that I actually look at my leg. It was a shock to see this monstrous limb and realize that it was attached to me. In stark contrast to my disbelief, the doctors were saying, "Doesn't it look good? Look what a nice stitching job we did."

My brain felt as if it were in slow gear, and I had to let the image of my leg seep into my mind only a bit at a time. The positive terms they were using to describe my leg were in total contradiction to what I was viewing. All I could see were stitches, scars, and flat areas where there should have been bumps. The shape alone wasn't even close to the shape of a normal leg. There was no calf, and my swollen knee and ankle made everything look more distorted. The skin graft that now covered the majority of my lower leg was full of permanent goose pimples, and it was a bright purplish-red color. It didn't look like human flesh; it looked like the skin of a chicken.

My leg wasn't there anymore. In its place was a mass of gross flesh that had been mangled. It no longer resembled any part of a human anatomy. It was a monster's leg. Any denial I had previously harbored about the seriousness of my injury was stripped away, and the reality of my injuries bombarded my mind. I could feel my body trying to reject what my eyes saw. My stomach turned into a rock, and my mouth dried as my throat closed off. I looked away, then tried just peeking in intervals to allow my body and mind some time for assimilation. Tears welled into my eyes as a deep sadness overcame me. I wished everyone would leave, which they did.

However, this direct visual encounter also had its positive side. Now that I could watch people work with my leg, I became more personally involved with its care. I was also allowed to go to physical therapy. Except for surgery I had not left my room since I arrived in May, and it was now June 28.

I went to P.T. on a flat cart. My leg was too unstable for me to ride in a wheelchair. Being transferred from the bed to the cart was painful, but it was exciting to venture out to new places. I lay on a mat that was lowered into a big whirlpool called a Hubbard Tank, which helped clean my leg and the rest of my body. It was wonderful to feel the water against my skin. I wished I could have a big sponge to scrub myself. The water felt as if it were washing away the heaviness collected on me during those hard weeks in the hospital. As I reclined in the tank, I could see the dead skin floating past my head, and I was concerned that it might stick to my hair. The Hubbard Tank was so pleasurable that I found myself hoping this would be a regular part of my therapy. I had always enjoyed being in water, so this deviation from my usual hospital day was great fun.

Sometimes I was embarrassed because my floating hospital gown didn't always cover me. The intern who assisted me in the Hubbard Tank was handsome, and I felt self-conscious about being exposed in his presence. His nonchalant attitude helped me feel more comfortable. He had the softest-looking long brown hair. One time when he was taking me down to the Hubbard Tank, he bent over me, and I almost reached up to try to touch his hair. I caught myself, but then I couldn't resist asking him if I could touch it.

He agreed, and I stroked his hair a couple of times. In the moment I felt silly and childish wanting to do something like this. I didn't realize that I was suffering from a form of deprivation. Only years later was it clear to me how natural my need really was.

As a patient with an open wound, I was always in a private room. I felt very lonely and isolated. Since I was in pain most of time, visitors—including my husband—didn't feel comfortable touching me. I didn't realize how much I needed to be touched and to touch someone in a nurturing way. Then one night I was awakened by a thunderstorm.

In my semiconscious state the sound of the thunder cracking instantly reminded me of my leg getting hit by the car. I woke up screaming. Two night nurses heard me and rushed in. I asked if either of them felt comfortable giving me a hug. I was crying and I felt scared by the memories of my accident. Both told me they did not feel comfortable hugging. I was surprised and hurt by their rejection. Despair filled my heart. My critical mind told me I was unworthy of affection and I was a fool to have asked. Nights like these—full of blackness and fear—added to my despair, and I was conscious of a deep ache in my heart.

The day after the thunderstorm, I called my friend Shirley. I confessed my need to be touched in a non-medical way. Later that day a wonderful woman came into my room. Netty was a nursing assistant and had heard from Shirley that I needed a hug. I received her hug with all my heart. Thereafter Netty came to visit me on a regular basis. Shirley, too, came to help, arriving the next day with a hug of her own.

Other than visiting the Hubbard Tank, physical therapy was done in my bed. My left leg was too unstable to be exercised, although I had gradually increased my ability to hold it up during examinations and bandage changes. I was given exercises to strengthen my arms and my right leg, using weights and the triangle that hung from my bed pole. I was highly motivated for these workouts: I would need strong limbs to maneuver a wheelchair or crutches.

Before my accident I was unaccustomed to sleeping on my back. It was difficult getting used to this new position. But as soon as the "lie as still as possible" orders were lifted, I found a way to sleep in a semisideways position, while still leaving my leg elevated.

It didn't take me long to realize that survival in a hospital depended on good nurses. General Hospital had an outstanding staff. Leading the long list who worked with me was Jane, a woman in her fifties. Clearly she liked nursing. She had been around a while and didn't hesitate to speak her mind—to patients or doctors. She took my chemical dependency seriously and was aware of my progressive dependency on morphine. I, too, knew in my heart that I had become dependent on this drug. It was obvious to me when I realized that I always started watching the clock in anticipation of my next injection.

The effects of morphine usually last three to four hours. My pain seemed to flare up and demand another shot right on schedule. Sometimes I was given too high a dose. I could tell because I would grind my teeth. When the dosage matched my pain level, I didn't experience as many side effects. I never protested when my dosage was too high; I only complained when it was too low. During this period when morphine was being prescribed for pain management, I couldn't gauge if I really needed it. My perspective became clouded with my addictive nature. My body cried out for morphine because it was time for another shot, whether I needed it or not.

I felt ashamed when Steve or members of my AA group visited and I was on pain medications. No one ever suggested I should stop taking the medications or that I was abusing them. But I could see the disappointment in Steve's eyes when he would come to visit and I was grinding my teeth and looking at him through a morphine glaze. It is impossible to fool another addict; I knew it and so did he.

After my skin-graft surgery, Jane suggested that it was time for me to stop the morphine. She offered me pain pills as a replacement. She put them within my sight but out of my reach, and she told me to call her if I felt I needed them. I was so scared and sure that an onslaught of massive pain was going to hit me. I trusted that Jane would give me the pain pills if I requested them, but I didn't think they would be strong enough. Surprisingly, as the day went on, I found that my pain didn't increase much. But I cried often for no apparent reason. I wasn't feeling sad, but the tears kept coming anyway. It was embarrassing. Later Jane told me she had seen this reaction among people who were withdrawing from morphine. Jane also told me later that the pain pills she had offered were just aspirin.

I found a new freedom from being off morphine. I

could think more clearly, and I felt more in control of my pain. But because morphine is such an effective manager of bone pain, the doctors continued to administer it to me immediately after every surgery. And there were many more surgeries ahead for me.

I went through a severe depression following every surgery. Part of the reason may have been constantly having to withdraw from morphine. Another part may have been my body's reaction to all the drugs administered during surgery. But Jane was always there to help me know when I no longer needed to use the morphine. Once it was given to me again, I could no longer make that decision myself. My addiction fooled me into thinking I could never live without it. When I was eventually released from the hospital, I prided myself on having stopped the use of all narcotics. On the other hand, I also felt a great deal of shame and guilt for having used them at all, since I was committed to sobriety.

So often it was the little things that made a big difference for me during the hospital recovery. Washing my hair was at the bottom of my nurses' agenda but at the top of my "things that make me feel good." Hair washing was a difficult task because I was unable to leave my bed. The procedure was messy, wet, and time-consuming. It required putting plastic on the floor and on my bed. A large plastic tray with a drainage spout was placed under my head. Pitchers of water were poured over my head to wet it and to rinse. This water was caught in a garbage can that had to be continually emptied. But getting my hair washed brightened my day.

Another thing to lift my spirits was to shave my healing leg. That task was considerably simpler than washing hair. Surprisingly, the hair on my left leg grew thicker and more quickly during the healing process. Before I noticed this, one visitor stated that it looked as if I were growing fur on that leg. After that, I was more conscious to keep it shaved.

On June 21 I.V. antibiotic treatment was discontinued for the first time since I arrived. This was a day to rejoice. In three weeks I had become an expert on I.V.s. Only the most experienced should attempt to put one in me. They hurt going in, and they lasted three days if all went well. "Pre-op" was the best place to get an I.V. because they usually got it in on the first try.

With no I.V., no fevers, and no pain medication, I regained some control of my life. I was still restricted to my bed, but I could use the bed pan independently, wash and feed myself, do assorted crafts, use the phone, and sleep better. Most of all, there were no painful procedures to anticipate.

I got to know the nursing staff quite well. At noon those who could steal a moment piled in my room and watched their favorite soap. When things were slow, they stopped in to visit, sometimes with a little trinket to cheer up my day, but always with the latest hospital gossip. Patients stopped in to visit, too, and they swapped horror stories with me. I became absorbed into the hospital community.

On June 28 a pressure sore developed on my heel. One part of the problem was that the blood circulation to my heel was poor. Another aspect of the problem was I had no feeling there. Consequently, I wouldn't notice that it was sore until the skin broke down. Usually this was recognized first by someone else. There was concern that a skin graft would be needed for it to heal. Various techniques were used to try to keep my heel off the bed so that it could mend. The creative Doctor Rothmen successfully invented a sling that I used for a long time to hold my foot up.

On July 17 the doctors took me into surgery once again to decorticate the bone in my leg—a procedure in which they chopped up the bone to help stimulate it to grow.

When I first awakened after surgery, I noticed green

stuff on my blankets. Then I started to vomit more of the same, which left a terrible, medicinal taste in my mouth. This continued for a few more hours. I asked one of the nurses why I was so sick and was told, "You are always sick after surgery." I never noticed that before, but in surgeries to come it proved to be true.

Going through this surgery meant being put back on I.V.s, back on morphine, and enduring another depression following the surgery. A few days afterward, I had a visitor from my AA group. Several of the members had come before and held AA meetings in my room for me. One member named Mary had not been able to attend those meetings. But she came alone this particular day because she was curious about the comments others had made about me. People had said I was an inspiration to visit in the hospital.

Mary was with me only a short time when she confronted me on my "Isn't it a miracle" story that I had repeated to all my visitors. She said, "How can it be that you don't feel angry about all this? I find that hard to believe. I think you're a phony."

I could feel embarrassment fill me. She was right on target. I was angry. I was tired of being prodded and poked and isolated from my family. I was also tired of being cheerful and cooperative. My attitude began to deteriorate as depression seeped in. Jane was the first staff member to notice and confront me on this. She suggested I needed some time alone with my husband. I agreed completely but didn't know how that could happen as long as I was in the hospital. Jane replied, "If Mohammed can't come to the mountain, let's bring the mountain to Mohammed."

I was shocked at her suggestion. "You think the doctors would allow Steve to come and be with me, here in the hospital?"

Jane told me, "It's been done before."

I worried about what people would think, including the doctors. Jane assured me she would talk to all the people who needed to know, and I should talk it over with my husband.

At first Steve felt shy about it, too. But the more we discussed it, the more excited we became. We got permission and set a date. The nursing staff put a sign on my door saying I was contagious and not to be disturbed without checking with the nursing staff. No vitals would be taken all night, and Steve was to attend to my personal needs.

You would have thought it was our first date. Steve felt so embarrassed because the staff knew he was there. We both were nervous about my leg. It still was unstable and had open wounds. Steve brought a great Mexican meal and a pie from the pastry shop. I hadn't eaten much since my hospitalization, so my stomach wasn't able to hold what my mind wanted. The food smelled great, and what's more it looked non-institutional. I loved it. After dinner we made love. Steve was nervous about my leg, and he handled me with care and tenderness.

Lovemaking had never been this wonderful in all the years of our marriage. We were both starved for nurturing. For the first time in our marriage, we put away our boxing gloves and allowed ourselves to be needy with each other. It was like I had always wished it to be. He stayed for a while and slept with me, but left early so he wouldn't meet any of the day shift nurses. He said it would be too hard to face them. It was odd that we should feel so shy about making love.

We were starting to build a new relationship. Being touched and feeling connected with Steve made me keenly aware of my desire to go home. My depression transformed into a motivation to go home. I started asking the doctors to find a way for that to happen. They finally came up with a plan. I was to learn how to care for my leg, and when I showed competence they would allow me to go home on a trial basis for a month.

One of the first obstacles that had to be overcome

was going from a bed to a chair. Being upright made me nauseated, and my bottom got sore sitting in the chair. Each day I extended my time in the chair, and then I graduated to a wheelchair with a leg extension. A wheelchair meant freedom. I visited other patients, and when Steve came to see me, he took me outside.

The first time I went outdoors I realized how much time had passed. The accident occurred in the spring; now it was summer. The trees were full of leaves, and the air was heavy with humidity. I was sure I would fall when Steve pushed me along the walkway. Every crack in the sidewalk was a threat. He laughed at me. I found it hard to adjust to the motion of the wheelchair, much less try to control how fast I went.

Looking up into the sky, I felt as if I could see forever. I had seen a ceiling for so long I had forgotten how expansive the sky was. Suddenly the isolation I had endured became more real to me. The fresh air filled me with a feeling of joy; it was the best medicine any doctor could prescribe. My heart was full of happiness and determination to leave the hospital as soon as possible. As much as I enjoyed my freedom, I found myself relieved when I returned to my room after that first outing. I was exhausted, and I wanted a safe place to be cared for.

Stephanie came to visit me for the first time when I was in the wheelchair. She had learned to walk while I was away, and she seemed so grown up since we were last together. She was scared of me when she first saw me. She clung to her daddy like a little monkey. My heart sank and I thought, "She doesn't know me." Finally her curiosity got the best of her. Very cautiously she sat on my lap. Little by little I could feel her guard come down until finally she let me snuggle with her. Oh, that felt so good! I had missed her so much!

I began to learn to clean my leg. Sterile bandage changes were not hard to master, and each part of the procedure I accomplished was a step toward going home. The doctors made a splint for my leg. It looked like a cast that had been cut in half. My leg set into it, and then an Ace bandage was wrapped around it to hold it in place. This device protected my leg, and I was instructed to wear it at all times except for cleanings.

Finally all I had to do was arrange for help once I was home. I received confirmation that a public health nurse would monitor my wounds and assist me in problem solving. I also asked some friends to stop by and check in on me, especially the first week.

With all the details taken care of, I was finally released. With me came bags of bandages and paraphernalia that I would need at home, plus a list of "dos and don'ts."

[10]

Riding home in the car I had motion sickness. I hadn't moved this fast in a long time. As we approached the house, I thought of how it looked the first time I saw it. We had been looking for a house to buy before Sherri was born. I was about seven months' pregnant, and Steve was on the road trucking. I was attracted to this house because it was located in an old neighborhood that felt welcoming. When I first saw it, I thought it was too good to be true. The owner wanted only $200 down and monthly payments of $200. I had expected a dump, and instead I found a small yellow stucco house that had a single garage and a large yard, situated on a corner lot. This house was originally a small farmhouse, with only a large kitchen and a bedroom off to the side. As time passed, additions had been put onto both sides of the kitchen—another bedroom, a bathroom, a dining room and living room, plus a porch.

It was our first home, and Steve had started several improvement projects throughout. It was his way of claiming the space as his, especially after his frequent absences during the trucking days. Consequently, certain areas of the house had an "under-construction look."

Steve took his time bringing me in that day that I returned from the hospital. We finally made it in the back door. I hadn't been home since May 28, and it was now July 31. I was exhausted. What I first noticed was the feeling that someone else had been caring for it. The only physical evidence I had was that things were arranged slightly differently. It didn't seem as if I had been missed; everything was orderly. But that was quickly replaced by a more positive feeling. I was engulfed with the warmth of my home. Someone else might have cared for it, but it still was my home and it was great to be back.

We put all the bandage paraphernalia in the bedroom, situated so that I could reach everything from my bed. Steve did not ask about my leg care or offer his assistance. It was as if a silent agreement had been made: my leg was my business. If I needed something, I was expected to ask—and preferably someone other than Steve. I suspect that he was insulating himself from my injuries. He had not processed his feelings about my leg at this time. I was used to fending for myself, so this invisible boundary was established without any resistance from me.

Using the wheelchair in our small home had its disadvantages. My left leg had to be elevated at all times, and an extension was attached to the wheelchair on which my leg could rest. This extension made it difficult for me to approach things directly, and it limited my mobility in any small area. It also restricted me to our bedroom, the kitchen, the dining room, and the living room. Accessing either the south section of the house or the porch on the north end both involved maneuvering one step. Therefore, I didn't have access to the bathroom, the girls' room, or the front porch. We had to rent a portable commode, which we kept in our bedroom.

Steve picked up the girls from day-care and cooked dinner. I had my first home-cooked meal in two months. At this meal I first realized the changes that had occurred in my absence. When Sherri and Stephanie sat down to eat, they appeared to be unusually quiet. Steve dished up the dinner: steak, potatoes, and green beans from the garden. I was amazed that Steve had time to grow vegetables this year. The girls stared at me, waiting for me to eat first. The meat was delicious, as were the potatoes. But when I put the green beans in my mouth, I realized they were too old to be eaten. They had become tough and woody. I put a mouthful of woody beans into my napkin and said, "Steve, this meal is wonderful. You've become a great cook while I was gone. I think you let the beans get a little too old before you picked them. I'm finding them a bit hard to chew."

Sherri said, "Are you going to eat your beans, Mommy?"

"No, I don't think I will, honey," I replied.

Sherri and Stephanie instantly livened up. "If Mom doesn't eat them, we're not going to either."

Steve flared, "You've just destroyed all my hard work. I have a rule around here that everybody has to clean her plate."

"Well, if you want me to clean my plate, you have to serve eatable food." Then I instantly regretted having spoken so harshly.

After dinner the impact of my day set in. Every part of my body hurt. The sting of my comments about Steve's meal was still in the air. To assist in clearing them away, I pushed my body fatigue away and offered to do the dinner dishes. Steve used to hate doing dishes, and I suspected that that had not changed. He was delighted that I offered and didn't hesitate to accept. I found I could manage the dishes by standing on one leg in front of the sink and resting my left leg on the back of the wheelchair, so as to keep it elevated. Eventually this was no problem, but that night I thought my right leg would give out at any moment from exhaustion.

When the girls were tucked in for the night, my heart sank that I couldn't be the one doing it. Even worse, they had grown accustomed to Steve tucking them in and didn't even question my absence.

Alone in our own bed, I told Steve it was obvious to me that he ran a much tighter ship than I ever had. The house was orderly, the girls were well behaved, and the laundry was cleaner than I had ever gotten it.

Steve told me he intended to continue doing laundry and grocery shopping because he could do it better than I could and he liked these jobs. I couldn't do laundry or groceries now anyway, but I could see that Steve meant even *after* I healed. It was different to see Steve take ownership of household chores. In the past he had never offered to help around the house.

That night it felt good to sleep in my own bed. I slept sounder than I had in a long time. In the morning Steve took the girls to day-care on his way to work. After he left, I did my bandage change and I got dressed. The head nurse at the hospital had told me to dress and wash up every morning, no matter how I felt. It would help protect me from depression.

I decided to reclaim my position in the house as cook and to surprise Steve with a four-star meal. I decided nothing less than a roast beef dinner would make the statement I needed to make. Preparing supper was a challenging adventure as I maneuvered around in a wheelchair, especially in this old house with its warped floors. Sometimes the wheel got stuck in a dip in the floor. Only my rage gave me enough energy to get myself unstuck.

Trying to reach items directly in front of me was difficult. Since my leg was extended straight out, it hindered me when I tried to get close to things. The occupational therapy staff had given me a pair of 18-inch tongs to assist this problem and they were invaluable. Sometimes I needed objects too high for anyone in a seated position. Then I stood on my right leg and kept my left leg elevated. The splint held it straight for me, and I could keep it up with one hand while I reached for objects with the other. This maneuver was eventually adapted so that I could hop across floors while holding my left leg out in front of me. A few times I slipped and came crashing down to the floor. I was usually more scared than hurt when this occurred.

By the time Steve got home with the girls, I was so exhausted I couldn't even eat the gourmet meal. Everything hurt, and I crawled into bed with promises to myself not to overdo it again.

My friend LeaRae was the public health nurse for my county. She stopped by frequently to check my wounds for signs of infection, to monitor my sterile bandage changes, and to problem-solve with me. One problem I had was emptying my portable commode. Steve repeatedly said he would empty it, but rarely did. Once when LeaRae came by, it was full to the top. I was so embarrassed that Steve had not taken care of it. I was also upset because I needed to use it, yet I was afraid it would overflow if I did. When LeaRae flushed its contents down the toilet, the plumbing clogged up and the backwash spilled out all over the bathroom floor. The carpeting was not attached to the floor, so LeaRae picked it up and took it to the basement to be washed later by Steve. It was quite a chore.

Being home wasn't as wonderful as I had thought it would be. The wounds on my leg were offensive to people, and I didn't receive positive feedback like I did in the hospital. There the staff made comments like, "Your leg is looking great today, Gayle." At home, people said, "Your leg looks gross. Does it hurt much?"

I kept my leg covered in bandages most of the time, even around my family. The girls adjusted quickly to the way my leg looked but were sensitive to how others perceived it. Steve kept his thoughts to himself but appeared guarded and separate from my wounds, as if he were trying to forget them. He treated me as if I were capable of fulfilling my roles as wife and mother. To him, leg care should not get in the way and the fact that the girls went to day-care was only a temporary measure, allowing me time to adjust.

People were busy with their own lives and, even though many people came to visit, a whole day would go by without any company. Steve and the girls were gone ten to twelve hours at a time. There was no community here for me. I also realized that the home I remembered was now Steve's home. He ran it, and the kids looked to him for their needs. I was an afterthought. I felt useless, and soon I started feeling depressed.

If I wanted to go to Al-Anon, I had to call someone who had a car big enough for my wheelchair. It was difficult getting me in and out of the house. There were some brave souls who assisted me, though. I hated having to ask for help all the time. I missed my independence and my old life.

At night, if one of the girls had a bad dream or cried out, I could not readily get to them. Steve was a much sounder sleeper than I, and he would not wake up to their cries. Before I learned to hop on one leg, I used to go to their rooms sliding my bottom across the floor.

Despite the pitfalls, I was still grateful to be home. It allowed for some measure of spontaneity in my life again. For example, one night Shirley and I went out to eat. We had the best time. Just as she was maneuvering me out of her car and into my wheelchair, it started to rain. I hadn't felt rain for a long time. I wanted to sit in it for a few minutes and feel it drop on my skin. Shirley said it was fine with her, but she was worried that I would catch a chill. The raindrops felt like fresh, cool kisses from heaven, revitalizing my spirit. When I got inside the restaurant, I felt chilled but my spirit was soaring.

I was involved in three support groups at this time: AA, Al-Anon, and my prayer and meditation study group. They were my lifelines. The people in these meetings were always glad to see me, and I could spend time focusing on something other than my leg.

Getting to AA was easier than Al-Anon because Steve went to an AA group of his own the same night and in the same building. Every Sunday evening Steve loaded the wheelchair into our car and carried me to it. Once we arrived, he unloaded the wheelchair, helped me into it, and pushed me into the building, which was a block from where we usually had to park. Steve never received any notice for all his labors; I would get all the attention once we came in because I was the one in the wheelchair.

My prayer and meditation study group conveniently met at my house. Fran (who had watched the girls for me the weekend of my accident) and LeaRae (my public health nurse) were part of the group, and it was here that our friendships began in 1976. At these study group meetings, we discussed reading material that assisted us in rais-ing our self-awareness and spiritual consciousness. From these meetings I learned meditation, the use of affirmations, and the rewards of self-discipline.

It is hard for me to discern prayer from meditation. To me the two are interconnected. Once I was told that prayer was speaking to God, whereas meditation was listening. These tools of worship allowed me to experience my God in a personal way. When I was in the receptive state of meditation, I found myself being filled with hope and with affirmation that I was not alone. I realized that my God knew what I needed and was responding. In my prayers I felt I had an effective voice in which to converse with my God. And I found myself telling Him my disappointments, fears, anger, desires, delights, and gratitude. I felt as if all messages were important and acceptable. My God was open to hearing my perceptions of His work, and I seemed able to hear His constant assurances of love.

Within two weeks of being home, Steve and I were invited to a party at Marie's house. Many of the bikers who had been with us Memorial Day weekend would be there. I didn't feel comfortable in large groups, and I usually didn't like parties for this reason. I was worried about being miserable once I got there. Steve, on the other hand, loved parties and thrived on the energy of large groups. Unfortunately, I never verbalized my concerns, and we went to the party.

When we got into the car, it wouldn't start. Steve informed me that the car had been having electrical problems. I suggested that maybe we shouldn't use the car if it was not working correctly. Steve told me not to worry, that he could fix it. After about thirty minutes, he had it running and we headed off to Marie's house.

Steve carried me into the party, leaving my wheelchair in the trunk of the car. He thought Marie's living room was too small for maneuvering a wheelchair. As we entered the party, I saw that Steve was right. He put me in a comfortable chair and went off to socialize while I just sat there. I felt uncomfortable receiving the amount of attention that came my way. People seemed relieved to see me out and about. My leg was the only subject they discussed with me that evening. I felt restricted sitting in that chair, not having the freedom to choose those to whom I wanted to talk.

After about two hours, I was tired and more than ready to go home. I asked Steve to take me home, but he wasn't ready to leave. We ended up staying until about 1:00 a.m. When we had traveled about a mile from the party, the car stalled in the middle of a busy intersection. It was closing time for the bars in that area, and there was a lot of traffic. It was a dark night, with only a few street lights along the way. When the car stalled, the headlights went out, too, making it difficult for approaching cars to see us until they were practically on top of us. The vulnerability of our situation sent a panic through me. The first car that came up behind us swerved violently to miss us, flipping on its two left wheels. It rolled past our car, then dropped down on all four wheels and kept going.

I was just thinking how lucky we were not to be hit by that car, when we were rear-ended by another. The impact sent my left leg smashing into the dashboard. Steve was furious. He got out of our car and started yelling at the folks who had just hit us. It was a carload of intoxicated women who were on their way home.

I felt terrified being in another accident so soon. It left me feeling paranoid. I thought someone was out to get me, and the angels weren't protecting me anymore. I also felt petrified to be left in the middle of the intersection in this car with no lights. I started screaming. Finally, someone came to my rescue. It was Marie. She and her husband had left the party to get more supplies and had come upon our accident. I asked Marie to get me out of the car and take me over to the grass where I would feel safe. She did, and I was able to calm down. I worried about my leg, but it was covered by my jeans so I couldn't assess the damage. By the sound it made when it hit the dashboard, I knew it must have been bruised. There was no pain (of course, I had no feeling in that part of my leg) or blood, so I felt the damage was minimal.

After the accident reports for the police were finished, Steve jump-started the car and we drove home. He said he was sorry my leg got hurt. This comment was intertwined with angry comments about how the police treated intoxicated women drivers differently from intoxicated men. When we got home, I removed the bandages and found that a part of the skin graft had been bruised and slightly torn. It eventually died.

A part of me became numb after the accident. Terror

was a new feeling for me, and it now filled every cell in my body. I felt that anything could happen to me because my God had forsaken me, my husband was incapable of protecting me, and I was dependent on others to have a life. I didn't know how to respond to the terror I felt, so a part of me shut down and my life went on automatic pilot.

As time passed, Steve and I adjusted to our new life style . He shared with me how alone he had felt while I was in the hospital. He was glad I was home and appreciated having someone to help with all the work. He told me one night that Wayne—one of the Memorial Day bikers—had come by to visit him. Steve said he was so grateful to have company that when Sherri fell asleep on his lap, he stayed put because he was afraid Wayne would leave if he got up. He even refrained from going to the bathroom until about midnight.

I could relate to Steve's loneliness. For years I had felt similar pain when he was trucking. I had often wished for help with all the work. Back then, I hoped Steve would someday feel alone, too. But hearing him tell about his feelings didn't give me the satisfaction I had fantasized. Instead I was being drawn closer to him by his new participation with the household and his sharing of feelings. It was very appealing and we felt more equal.

Sherri's fifth birthday arrived around the same time I was to be readmitted into the hospital for more surgery on my leg. I planned a party a little early so that I could celebrate with her. Everything was set for when she got home from school. I had gone to Al-Anon that morning with the help of Judy, one of my friends from the group. Stephanie stayed with me that day because she had a cold. We had just returned from Al-Anon when I noticed that Stephanie's breathing was labored. Eventually I became concerned enough to call Judy and ask her to come back and take us to a doctor.

By the time Judy arrived, Stephanie's lips and nails had a blue tinge. As she lay in my arms, she became limp. I got panicky. Judy quickly packed us into her car, wheelchair and all, and took us to the doctor.

The doctor gave Stephanie a shot that should have helped her breathe more easily, but it didn't work. After a few more attempts with medication, she told me that Stephanie would have to be admitted to the hospital.

I called Steve's workplace and left a message for him to come home. Not knowing if he would get there in time for Sherri's party, I called my neighbor and asked her to help out. Thinking that it was too much to ask of one person, I also called my brother's wife. Meanwhile, the doctor informed me that Stephanie had pneumonia and possibly asthma. They put Stephanie into a crib with an oxygen tent. She looked very small and vulnerable lying there, struggling for every breath. Judy told me she had an asthmatic child and it was hell. She said she had suspected asthma when she saw Stephanie's breathing.

When Steve arrived at the hospital, he was angry. The message he had received said that his daughter was in the hospital. He had no idea which daughter or what the problem was. He had decided to go to the house first, where he found several adults trying to organize Sherri's party, and it was chaotic.

I explained what the doctor had said about Stephanie's condition and that I intended to stay the night with her. I had already requested that a bed be brought into her room and was granted permission to stay all night. Steve replied that he was going back to work and didn't understand why I had to stay all night with Stephanie.

My arms hurt as I watched a nurse shove the I.V. into Stephanie's little arm. I hovered over her, protecting her from my imagined fears—worries created by my own experience in the hospital. Steve's last angry words echoed in my mind: "Why do you have to stay here? I want you at home."

I felt defeated, scared, and alone. The hospital had not wanted me to stay. I was one more inconvenience to them. Stephanie appeared unaware of my presence. She slept through the night, her breathing labored. My body ached from the exertion of the day, and I needed to care for my leg. The staff gave me the supplies I needed, but I knew they were burdened by my requests. My insides cried out for someone to tell me everything was going to be O.K. There was no one to comfort me.

Stephanie ended up staying a few nights in the hospital. I went home after the first night.

When Stephanie was discharged, asthma was diagnosed. Up to this point, we had seen whatever doctor was available when we came into the clinic. But Stephanie's doctor this time suggested that we contact her specifically if we needed further medical help. She wanted Stephanie to have consistent care. I was grateful for this doctor's concern, and she regularly cared for Stephanie for the next year.

[11]

On September 17, 1979, I returned to the hospital for a bone graft. It was a new experience to be admitted into the hospital when I felt healthy. It would become a familiar one.

I was asked to sign permission slips that gave the hospital the freedom to choose procedures and gave me the right to know their choices. An identification band was put on my wrist. Even though it was made of plastic, it felt like a shackle. I was then wheeled to my room and introduced to the new medical student assigned to my case.

Medical students were not a positive experience for me. I was always given a new one with each admission. They would enter my room looking overwhelmed and tired. Typically, the first thing they would say was, "How's your foot?"

It was easy to understand this inappropriate remark. From the accident my foot had a large scar on it—a huge stretch mark left after previous swelling receded. My foot was also discolored from the lack of circulation, and its top was so hypersensitive that I didn't like the feeling of a sheet. So when the medical student came in, my foot was exposed but my leg was covered.

If medical students asked about my foot, I knew that they had not read my chart. This again was understandable because my chart was very thick, and the students were chronically short on time. But their question destroyed any credibility they might have had with me.

I would respond, "My foot is fine. It's my leg that has given me all the trouble." Then the medical students would give me a physical exam that was methodically done, exactly as their textbook had taught them. If there was any chance of salvaging the relationship, it often was lost when it came time for an I.V. to be inserted. Even though I would explain that when an I.V. was inserted into the back of my hand, the veins had always collapsed, most medical students disregarded what I said and proceeded to try to prove me wrong. Their books taught them to start all I.V.s low in the arm, so when the vein collapsed they were to graduate up the arm, thus prolonging the use of arm veins. After collapsing the veins in each hand, the students would travel up my arm, repeatedly failing to insert the I.V. Eventually the assigned intern would be called in to help. But by the time the I.V. was successfully inserted, I had been poked several times. As my hospitalizations continued, my anxiety toward I.V.s increased. I remember one doctor saying to me, "I don't understand why people make such a big deal about I.V.s. I had one once and it hardly hurt at all." I instantly fantasized that this doctor was the guinea pig for all the medical students.

The only medical student I remember fondly was Bob. He was assigned to me during my first hospitalization. Perhaps we had a chance to form a positive relationship because he never had to undergo this initial admissions process with me. He was studying to become a pathologist, so he liked tissue that was already dead. Often he would spend an hour calmly cutting dead tissue from my wounds. This was a painless but tedious task. We got acquainted during those lengthy sessions. Bob told me that healing my leg would be a long process, and it would require many surgical procedures. Those long talks with Bob helped me break through my denial of the wounds. Our conversations allowed me to start preparing myself for what was ahead. Years later when I read my medical charts, I found these closing remarks about our time together:

> Gayle Martinez is a young married woman with kids who was riding on a cycle with her husband on 5/28/79, when a passing car caught her left leg . . . Her hospital stay will probably be at least another 3-4 weeks 'till her wound heals better.
>
> Gayle is a very rewarding person to take care of, as she appreciates everything you do for her. She will instruct you on how to move her leg around when you irrigate so it does not hurt. Gayle tends to freak out every once in a while, especially with any change, but can be talked down from this.
>
> Good Luck, Bob

But Bob was a rarity, at least as far as I could tell. For this particular admittance—the September bone graft—my admissions check-up from a medical student was pretty typical. Next I was prepared for surgery. The purpose of the procedure was to clean my leg and make it as ready as possible for the imminent bone graft. Unfortunately, the cultures taken from my wound indicated a staph infection was present. I was put on I.V. antibiotics immediately. Following surgery I had my usual reaction of prolonged nausea and depression. Morphine was also administered for a short time.

Doctor Rothmen—one of the emergency room physicians the night of my accident—was now the resident doctor assigned to my case. He was very handsome, and the nurses fell all over him. As before, I found him hard to talk to. I also missed Doctor Lindqueist. When Doctor Rothmen came into my room, which was as infrequently as possible, he always appeared preoccupied with something else. When I asked him why he never came to see me, he answered that my smoking bothered him. Then he lectured me about the hazards smoking had on my healing process. This left me feeling defensive and guilty.

Before going in for the bone graft, Steve and I had discussed a tubal ligation. It was scary for me to think of becoming pregnant and carrying a baby with my leg so unstable. I also worried that harm might have been done to my reproductive system by the extensive use of X-rays and medications. I discussed all this with Doctor Rothmen to see if it was a good idea to consider having a tubal ligation at the same time as my bone graft. He checked and later told me there would be no problem combining the surgeries.

While waiting for these operations, I was allowed to participate in physical therapy (P.T.). This time I arrived in my wheelchair, ready to do more than lie in a Hubbard Tank. The first thing I noticed upon arriving was a number of unhappy old people. Many of them were crying, and their tears reminded me of those that came after I had been taken off morphine. When I asked one of the therapists about their tears, he said, "They always do that. They don't want to be here. They don't want to work on their recovery." I couldn't imagine why anyone wouldn't want to be in physical therapy. It didn't make sense to me that people wouldn't want to work on recovering.

My wheelchair was put into a line with other wheelchairs waiting to go into P.T. As I got closer to the therapy room, I could hear people crying out in pain. I started to feel anxious.

Finally a therapist was assigned to me. Jenny was a perky woman who had just graduated from the university. I was one of her first patients, and she was anxious to get my leg back in shape.

Jenny helped me into a chair that was attached to a small whirlpool, a tub just big enough for my leg. Water therapy was used to help my muscles relax before working on increasing my range of motion. My leg had become stiff from being held straight and elevated for the past four months. The doctor had ordered only passive exercises because my tibia was still in two pieces. After the whirlpool, I lay on a mat, and my injured leg was hung over a stick. Gravity pulled my leg down, causing my knee to bend. A few other exercises were also done to strengthen my good leg and loosen my hips.

My first experience in P.T. was positive, so I couldn't understand why the other people were unhappy. My mind tried to blame morphine, but my heart suspected I had a lot to learn.

During this hospital stay, I noticed that fewer visitors came. Actually it was a more manageable number of people now. My AA group came and had meetings with me. They told me that they cared about me, and I believed them. I felt nurtured when they came and shared their hearts with me.

During this time I noticed a change in the relationship with my father. Until now, my father and I had never been close. When I was a child, he was unavailable to me while he concentrated on building his business. When I was an adolescent, my parents divorced and my father remarried soon after the final papers were signed. I carried resentments both about how this was handled and toward my father's new wife. It was as if the relationship between father and daughter had never had time to form.

But since my accident, he had taken a real interest

in my healing process. He came to see me regularly, encouraged me, and applauded my perseverance. It was wonderful to have my dad participate in my life. I was grateful for his attention—and surprised.

My September hospitalization wasn't my first bone graft. The first one had been tried during my initial hospitalization, but it had not been successful. The word I heard was: bone grafts are painful. The surgeons use bone from one part of the body to stimulate bone growth elsewhere. Their plan was to use bone from my right hip. It was explained to me that the top of the bone is chipped off to obtain a liquid-like substance, which would then be scooped out and put into my left leg, where the tibia needed to grow together.

On September 25 I had this surgery along with a tubal ligation. When I returned to my room, I experienced pain in my right hip, nausea, and a terrible cramping in my intestinal area. I found out later that when performing a tubal ligation, the doctors fill this area with gas to make it more accessible. Normally women walk around shortly after this surgery, and the motion helps to release any gas trapped in the intestines. But I was flat on my back and had been given orders to "lie as still as possible." These orders—given to maximize the success of the bone graft—didn't help my recovery from the ligation.

In short: these two procedures required opposite maintenance. Since the bone graft took precedence, I lay as still as possible. The pain of the trapped gas and the nausea from the surgical medications created a nightmare I hope never to repeat.

I stopped taking morphine as soon as Jane gave me the word and went through three days of depression, preoccupied with suicide. The depressions I had experienced following other surgeries hadn't been as deep as this one. I felt enveloped in darkness and incapable of reaching out for help. Time passed and it lifted. I realized this despair was not new to me. It felt similar to what I endured after using street drugs and alcohol. Since becoming sober, I had often struggled with fully admitting and accepting my alcoholism. Compared to Steve or other alcoholics, my drinking didn't have consequences like theirs. I often said to myself, "I never smashed up a car, I was never arrested. So how could I be called an alcoholic?" And when I got depressed after bouts with chemicals, I always thought it was because of Steve's behavior.

He couldn't be blamed for my despair this time. As I lay in the hospital bed recovering from the bone graft, I realized that my despair might be connected with using drugs. This not only made sense but it validated my addiction for me. Only addicts continue to use a substance that makes them feel despair. Now I was starting to understand the consequences of my addiction. Once again I was forced to look at my own behavior instead of Steve's.

Osteomyelitis was discovered in my leg—a prolonged bacterial infection of the bone. It takes a long time to formulate and an equally long time to cure. Osteomyelitis is the number-two reason for amputation—second only to accidental amputation. The treatment for me was largely preventative: three weeks of I.V. antibiotics after every surgery. This was tough. My veins weren't holding up well to these I.V.s. I requested oral antibiotics and was told oral antibiotics were not strong enough to fight this infection.

Several days after the bone graft, the bandages were removed from the donor site on my hip. I was surprised to see two incisions instead of one. I asked about this constantly, and finally Doctor Rothmen came in and told me he had done the surgery. When he cut me the first time, it had been in the wrong location. He stood at the end of my bed, nervously bouncing from one foot to the other. He looked at me and said it was a mistake, and that he was sorry. It was the only time I saw Doctor Rothmen vulnerable. I accepted his apology and never mentioned it again.

Prayer was an important aspect of this hospital stay. Many people were still praying for me, and Beth was still sending me healings. One of the orderlies who took me to surgery was a born-again Christian. When we were alone in the elevator, he asked if he could pray for me; I said yes. During my recovery Steve arrived with a couple who came to pray with me. I found this embarrassing because I didn't know them, and Steve and I had never prayed together. It felt awkward in front of strangers to pray with Steve for the first time. I tried to stay present during the prayer, thinking, "It couldn't hurt." After they left, Steve asked me what I thought of his bringing this couple to pray with us. I told him it was O.K. He said, "Well, I figured it couldn't hurt."

I was released on October 13 with orders to be back in December.

[12]

It was good to be home again. The air was crisp with fall. Halloween was just around the corner. Sherri was excited, and so was I. Stephanie was too young to understand the holiday, but she picked up that something fun was going on. I loved to see the neighborhood kids coming to the door, dressed up in their costumes. For the previous couple of years, I had gone to a few neighbors and given them assorted sugar-free treats intended for Sherri when she came "trick or treating." I had limited Sherri's sugar intake since she was two years old because she had been reactive to it. This year it was up to Steve to prepare the neighborhood for Sherri's "trick or treating," and he did.

When Halloween night came, Steve and Sherri were out for a long time. When they walked in, Sherri wore a grin that went from ear to ear. They were full of stories and candy. Sherri told me that they had made a deal, deciding to stay out as long as they could and go to houses that she had never gone to before. Then, when they got home, Daddy would get to keep the candy with sugar in it, and she could have what was left. This deal seemed like a good one to Sherri because she had so much fun being out late with Daddy.

The autumn seemed to move quickly. The girls were home with me full-time now, except for Sherri's morning kindergarden. Often the girls were excellent helpers; other times, they would get just out of my reach and refuse to help at all. During these rebellious episodes, I became angry at my limitations. And anger wasn't my only troubling emotion. Sometimes I would break down in tears of frustration from being unable to accomplish a simple task like changing a crib sheet.

I had lost control of so many aspects of my life. The pieces were slow to come back. And when they returned, they had changed. My leg took up most of my energy, and what was left over was used to help around the house. Steve was very involved with both the kids and housekeeping. There was no longer a need for me to be a super mom. What did that make me now? What was my role in life now?

On Sunday mornings a group of healers met at Beth's house. I went one Sunday, accompanied by a friend. Up to this point I had only a vague idea what Beth looked like; we had never formally met. Her house appeared old and small to me, but it felt homey and safe inside. I noticed chairs had been set up in the living room, arranged in a large circle with several additional ones in the center. A group of people were standing around chatting. I looked for Beth. She spotted me first and introduced herself. She had white hair, a soft face, and a twinkle in her eye. Her welcoming grin told me she was thrilled that I could make it. I couldn't wait to feel her healing hands on me.

Everyone took seats. The healing service began with a prayer and a period of meditation. Then various people went to the chairs that had been placed in the middle of the room. As they sat down, others stood behind them and began doing healings. I moved toward the center in my wheelchair, praying that Beth would be my healer. A pair of soft warm hands were placed on my shoulders. I recognized her touch immediately. Tears filled my eyes as her energy began to flow through me. Afterward we hugged.

Later Beth told me I had felt familiar to her, too. I knew I was blessed to have her as my healer. Thereafter she continued to send me absentee healings, until I was able to transport myself to her home for private healing sessions. The bond between us will always run deep. I am so very grateful for her commitment to healing and to me.

Time went by so quickly now that I was home. Thanksgiving arrived and offered another opportunity for family celebration. This year Steve's sister, Linda, offered to cook the Thanksgiving meal. For many years I had shared Thanksgiving with Steve's family. His mom, Marge, had cooked most of the Thanksgiving dinners. Marge had been my surrogate mom right after Steve and I married. She helped me learn about house cleaning and shared recipes with me. When Sherri was born, she was the person I called to help me learn parenting. Her death from cancer in 1977 was a great loss to us all. Whenever we gathered for a holiday, she was still very present.

One of the few Thanksgiving meals not prepared by Marge was cooked by me. That year Steve invited a couple to be our guests. We had been married about a year and were living in a double bungalow in the Midway area of St. Paul.

This was my first Thanksgiving meal preparation, and I had started early that morning by taking the turkey out of the freezer. We had set up a card table in the living room because our kitchen had room for only two. All afternoon I was busy making things. I could see the turkey was having trouble thawing out, so I decided to cook it still frozen. Dorean and Chris came over about 6:00 just as the potatoes and corn finished cooking. Much to my surprise the turkey was still raw. By 8:00, the guys had given up on my turkey ever getting done. They went out to a bar. Chris and I stayed home and ate cold potatoes and salad.

Since that experience I had learned to respect the timing, effort, and knowledge required to cook successfully a big meal. So when Linda offered to cook Thanksgiving dinner, I was appreciative. I was also glad to be with Steve's relatives, including his dad. It was a place where Marge would be remembered. The men watched football while my girls enjoyed their cousin Robby, who was a few years younger than they. We all enjoyed Linda's meal and were grateful to share this time together. I had so much to be thankful for: sobriety, family, new beginnings, loving memories, and no I.V.s.

[13]

On December 3, 1979, I returned to the hospital. Steve and the girls went to admissions with me. As the plastic wrist band was being attached to my arm, I became overwhelmed with emotional pain. I did not want to be back. My heart felt as if it would burst wide open from despair. The image that filled my mind was one of being in a prison. In the hospital I was to be isolated from any nurturing touch and fresh air; various potions were administered to me that induced vomiting and hallucinations; and I was to be exposed to professionals who manipulate my body parts utilizing hammers, saws, and drills. But the worse part about coming back was my loss of control.

Sherri asked why I was crying. Steve told her, "Mommy's sad about coming back to the hospital."

I asked Steve to leave because I couldn't pull myself together. I didn't want to scare Sherri or Stephanie. He left and I was wheeled to my room.

I sat on my bed and tried to prepare myself for the upcoming surgery. It was scheduled for the next morning. Out of the corner of my eye, I thought I saw my mom walking past my door. A cold chill ran down my spine. She had said she had a surprise for me, but it was hard to believe that she would come unannounced. My heart sank. My mom lived in the state of Washington. She moved there a few years after she divorced my dad. My history with her had taught me that whatever she was able to give was temporary and on her own terms.

When I was hospitalized in May, she called and told me she would connect with me every day to give me support. She told me she was saving her visit for when I needed her the most. Although I was suspicious of her offer, it was so appealing that I allowed myself to believe it. In fact we talked on a regular basis during my first hospitalization, and I kept her updated on the latest procedures being done to me. When it became possible for me to go home in July, I asked my mom to come and help me. She got angry at me for asking and suggested that I had tricked the doctors into an early release. She was sure I was jeopardizing the recovery of my leg just because I wanted to be with Steve. Seeing her brought back the pain of this event and others like them. How could I handle both being back in here *and* a visit from my mom? The Lord does work in mysterious ways.

She entered my room with a grin on her face. I felt my face go into its automatic grin and tried to welcome her sincerely. As it turned out, my surgery was delayed a day, and it was a nice distraction to have my mom there. She played word and card games with me to help pass the time.

I was taken into surgery the next day. The plates that had been put in my leg originally to hold it together had become infected. Now they were being removed. After surgery, I was surprised to find two new wounds. On the back of my leg was a long incision that had been stitched. On the front was another long incision that remained open. My doctor explained that my leg didn't have enough skin to close this wound. It would have to fill in on its own by growing new tissue. This would take a long time and require constant attention.

Steve came to visit the first night after my surgery. He had a diaper bag in one hand, Stephanie in the other, and Sherri alongside of him. My mom thought it was great that Steve had all this responsibility and congratulated herself for not coming out sooner to help. She reasoned that if she had come, it might have interfered with Steve becoming so involved with the children. Steve was livid that she was in town and had not even offered to help him; I was angry and frustrated at my mom's limitations.

I was to have another surgery the next day in which a Hoffman fixator was to be put on my leg—an external structure attached with pins that went all the way through my leg. Its purpose was to stabilize my leg so the bone could heal. The most exciting advantage it offered me was the ability to walk with crutches.

As usual, food and drink were not allowed after midnight when surgery was scheduled for the next morning. Having just had surgery the day before, I hadn't felt much like eating that day. Then food and water were stopped at midnight. The next morning I woke up feeling apprehensive about the surgery. Again I was glad my mom was there to entertain me and help me pass the time. It was a long day. Around 7:00 that evening I was told the surgery had been postponed another day. I had permission to eat and drink, but the kitchen was closed. The nurses dug up some juice, crackers, and a candy bar. Food and liquid were stopped again at midnight.

By the morning—now the 7th of December—my anxiety level had doubled. I asked one of the nurses why my surgery had been postponed twice during this admittance. She told me that I used to be a priority surgery because many of my procedures were emergencies. I no longer had priority status if an emergency arrived, and they had had several during the last few days. She reassured me that they would get me in that day.

I could feel a total dependence on my mom forming as the day progressed and my surgery didn't happen. We had played games continually. I was panicky that she would leave, and I wouldn't have her as a diversion anymore. I smoked incessantly, and without liquids the smoking caused me to have dry heaves occasionally. When evening arrived, I was very irritable and felt as if I could crawl out of my skin. My surgery was again postponed until morning. I was told I could eat, but again the kitchen was closed, so the nurses scrounged up more tidbits from their refrigerator. At midnight all food and liquids were prohibited. I awoke on the third morning awaiting surgery. My anxiety level had reached an all-time high, but my mom stuck with me until they finally came and got me just before noon.

I awoke with a Hoffman fixator attached to my leg and the news that my mom had left. I felt her visit had helped to heal my anger, and the most forgiving part of me realized she had given me every ounce she was able to give. The little girl part of me hated that she was not able to be what I needed her to be: a consistent parent. In retrospect, it seems that perhaps she really did come to see me when I needed her the most; it just wasn't when I asked her to come.

The device on my leg had six pins that went through my leg—each was about the width of the wire used in a heavy clothes hanger. Three pins were just below my knee and three were above my ankle. They were attached to thicker rods that went vertically down each side of my leg. It was a strange-looking device, but painless.

Each day a nurse came to irrigate my open wounds and clean the area where the six pins went through my leg. It was a painless procedure but time-consuming.

Soon they taught me to do it for myself.

When I was home the previous time, Marie took me shopping for new bib overalls. I found that they were easy to pull on over my leg splint and comfortable when sitting around in my wheelchair. Now I asked Marie, who was handy with a needle and thread, if she would devise a method of altering my bibs so they would fit over this new contraption. She put extra material on the bottom of my left pants' leg so that it had a large bell-bottom. Then she attached snaps that went completely up the side so I could easily get them on. It was pure genius in my eyes.

Another surprise after this surgery was finding an I.V. in my chest. The doctors told me it could last a couple of weeks. What a relief! And it was painless. They had inserted it while I was under anesthesia, and it was long-term. I felt as if things were looking up.

On December 11, I developed a stiff neck, and my right ear hurt. The nurses thought it was caused by a draft from my window, but it turned out to be from the chest I.V. It had been inserted into a vein that came down through my neck. It wasn't the vein they had hoped it was in, and now the vein was breaking down. My doctors diagnosed it as phlebitis of the right internal jugular. What it meant to me was I.V.s back in my arms.

Also on December 11, I was sent to P.T. to learn crutch walking. I was greeted by my peppy physical therapist, Jenny. She was now able to do more strenuous exercises with me because of my Hoffman fixator. She put my leg in a whirlpool and left me to loosen up my muscles. When she returned she said, "Now let's see if we can get that knee to bend."

With one swift movement she cranked my leg down, and my knee bent almost forty-five degrees. Cracking noises came from that joint as the adhesions that had formed tore loose. Stabbing pains shot through me and my eyes filled with tears. Jenny said, "Isn't that great? We have some significant movement now." The look on my face must have registered what she had done to me, and she added, "Why don't you stay in the whirlpool for a while and we'll call it a day."

I now understood why people didn't like P.T. It had changed from an exciting place to recover into a challenging place to survive. In my future P.T. visits, I became an expert at distracting physical therapists. Timing was essential to lessen my pain. I found that if I could make the therapist laugh just before they attempted to "improve my range of motion," their laughter weakened the attempt. One of my tactics was to say in a little voice, "Oh, no, Mr. Bill. No! No!" This was taken from a comedy show on television at the time. My ploy was very effective.

December 17 was my twenty-eighth birthday. My friend Donna came to visit. We were born on the same day and had known each other since we were fourteen, but this was the first birthday we were able to celebrate together. She brought me a small chocolate cake, which we delightfully consumed as we talked.

I was to be released the night of December 21. While waiting for Steve to arrive, the doctor told me that before sending me home he had to clean up the wound on the front of my leg. The bone was exposed there, and some dead fragments remained that could hinder the healing process.

He put my leg up on a pillow and started cutting off bits of my bone with a pair of clippers that looked as if they could be used to trim a horse's nails. Every time he clipped I could feel my bone vibrate, and the sensation was similar to fingernails scraping a chalkboard. As pieces of bone and blood dotted the sheets around me, I was overcome with a feeling of being violated. The thought that pieces of me were being chopped up was too much for my mind to process. I started yelling for him to stop. He asked if it hurt, and I said, "Not exactly." I just didn't want him to do it any more. He told me if I didn't let him continue with the debridement, I would need to be anesthetized, which would postpone my discharge until the next day.

I didn't want more drugs or more time in the hospital, so I let him continue, but I kept screaming. When the doctor finally finished, he was frazzled. He just walked out, and I was left alone with my leg and bits of bone all around me. The nurse came in after what seemed like an eternity and cleaned up the mess. Soon after the nurse left, Steve came in, excited to see me on crutches. My whole body was shaking, and he said, "I don't want to know what happened. I just want to get you home."

We left with bandages and supplies and orders to report to the orthopedic clinic after the holidays.

[14]

There were only a few days before Christmas and lots of shopping to be done. Although I had crutches, I used my wheelchair on long trips. Steve took me to a shopping mall near our house to look for presents. It was fun to be out in the stores. Even though my energy didn't last as long as I had hoped, we got most of our shopping done. This was the first time Steve and I had ever gone Christmas shopping together. We both realized we liked doing it this way.

It was a quiet Christmas time. We spent Christmas Eve at our house, a tradition I had tried to establish the last few years. Shirley came over and helped me make some appetizers and donated some of her famous cheese balls. Any other year I would have been baking for weeks in preparation for the Christmas Eve dinner. This year Steve was the main cook, and he did a fine job preparing a meal for the occasion. My brother and his family stopped by, as did Steve's sister and her family, Steve's dad, and my dad and his wife. Steve got lots of attention for preparing the meal, and I was glad I hadn't tried to do it.

On Christmas Day we went over to my dad's house for a while. My energy ran out quickly, and we returned home to finish our Christmas quietly.

The new year brought with it a new experience for me: orthopedic clinic. On January 15, I entered the hospital through this new door. Clinic was to become a big part of my life. Nancy, a wonderful lady from my study group, took me to clinic. She had spent many years with one of her sons in clinics like this one. She offered her services immediately when she saw the need arise. I wondered why someone who had gone through all this before would choose to go through it again. If the opportunity arose, I didn't think I would jump at the chance. But she did, and she continued to do so for a long time to come.

Clinic was usually in the morning for me. It entailed waiting for about an hour in a crowded reception area before being taken into an examination room. After another long wait, I was examined. Then I was put in line with several other people to have X-rays taken of my leg. Next I was brought back to the examination room, where I waited to see my doctor. Finally, Dr. Gustillo would examine my leg and discuss the X-rays with me.

I liked Dr. Gustillo because he seemed to care about me as a person. He was the head of the orthopedic ward and had been in charge of my case since the beginning. I hadn't gotten to know him in the hospital because he wasn't as personally involved with me there. Other staff had told me that he was one of the best orthopedic doctors around, and I was lucky to have him on my case. It didn't take me long to trust him and believe what I had heard about him.

On my first clinic visit, Dr. Gustillo told me the X-rays showed that the two previous bone grafts had not been successful. My tibia bone was still in two pieces and showed no indication of growing together. He suggested that the tibia bone could be dead. If so, nothing more could be done and amputation would be the best course of action. There was a test that would indicate if the bone was still alive; he scheduled it for January 31.

My reaction to this news was a strong sense that life *was* present in my tibia. The possibility of my bone being dead was not even in my consciousness. I saw that the difficulty would be to pass the test so that the doctors would know what I already knew in my heart.

I scheduled a healing with Beth a few days before I was to go in for this test. She understood the significance of what was coming up. Before she began the healing, she asked for help from Mother-Father God, the angels, the White Brotherhood, and all those who were surrounding me with their light and assisting me in healing. When she put her hand over the spot on my tibia where there was a non-union, I felt an incredibly intense heat that seemed electrically charged. It entered my leg where her hand was, but it permeated my entire being. The whole experience was powerful and moving. We both acknowledged that a tremendous healing force had entered my body. There was no doubt in my mind that I would pass this test about which Dr. Gustillo was so concerned.

On January 31 I went to clinic. I passed the test with flying colors! Dr. Gustillo was pleased to tell me there was plenty of life registering from my tibia. He suggested the other bone grafts hadn't taken because my leg had been constantly fighting off infections, and the area of non-union was never completely stabilized. He felt that with the Hoffman fixator my leg was now stabilized; and, since I didn't have an infection at the time, he suggested I come into the hospital and have another bone graft.

Dread instantly replaced the joy of passing the test. Bone grafts were painful and would require another three weeks in the hospital.

[15]

I was re-admitted on February 11 and introduced to my new medical student. He entered my room and asked, "Well, how's your foot doing?"

All the rest of what followed has been said before. Little had changed on the orthopedic ward except my three new doctors. After each of them had examined me, I was pleasantly surprised by a fourth doctor's visit. He was an anesthesiologist. He told me that he had been reviewing my chart and saw that I had struggled with post-operative nausea. He thought that I was reacting to sodium pentothal.

We discussed my options, and he left with a new plan of action. He intended to put together a series of medications that he would use during the surgery in hopes of lessening my nausea.

What a miracle that this man cared enough to come and discuss this with me. What's more, he also told me I had a right to request a visit from the anesthesiologist who would be involved with any of my future surgeries. I was grateful for this piece of information and planned to use it.

Fortunately my surgery went well, and bone cells were taken from my left iliac crest (an area just above my left buttock) and put into my left tibia at the area of non-union. I found that by the end of the day my nausea had receded—a blessing compared to previous anesthesia reactions. Everyone felt that the surgery had been a huge success.

When I returned from surgery, I was surprised to find myself with a roommate. A young girl who had also suffered a leg injury. She had returned to have the Schneider nail removed from her femur. I knew that this was a procedure I would have to have done someday, since I had a Schneider nail, too. The good news was that she would be in the hospital only thirty-six hours: admitted that night, surgery the next day, and released the day after that.

I was shocked to see her after her surgery. She was ready to eat and visit. She ordered a hamburger for lunch. Her family arrived with homemade treats and cold washcloths for her forehead. They were quiet, respectful, and emotionally there for her. She told me that her dad had saved all the paraphernalia used on her leg and had created a display wall in their house. Her father had found her recovery inspiring, and the display was an affirmation of her strength and persistence.

Despair was my reaction to this show of nurturing. I pulled the curtain between us closed, hoping for some semblance of privacy as I tried to muffle my sobs. Sharon entered at that moment and wheeled me out of the room. She was a counselor I had started to see while I was in the hospital. I was aware that I had an enormous amount of resentment building up from my hospital stays. I also believed these resentments could hinder my recovery. As it turned out, Sharon had arrived just in the nick of time. We found a quiet room, and I sobbed and sobbed. Those tears were for myself and for all that I had gone through: the lack of consistent support and the absence of the personal touch triggered by my new roommate. Sharon held my hand and let me sob. I was so grateful.

Of course, once the dam broke, I had the weepies all day. My roommate and her family were very concerned, but I found no words to tell them about my pain. They respectfully left me alone. The nursing staff also showed concern. But with the lack of privacy in my room, I felt I couldn't voice my pain to them either. These feelings passed as soon as the girl left to go home. Watching her go through her surgery left me with some hope, however. When the doctors were to remove my Schneider nail, it would only be a short hospitalization and a simple procedure.

During my previous hospitalizations, I had had only one roommate: Betty. She was nicknamed the "bionic woman." Betty was in her sixties, and she had spent most of her life living in hospitals. When she was a teen-ager, everyone in her family had gotten ill from drinking non-pasteurized milk. All except Betty recovered from the illness, and she developed arthritis throughout her body. As was customary in those days, she was given a room in the hospital in which to live because of her constant medical needs. By the time I was introduced to her decades later, many of her joints had been replaced with artificial ones, including those in her wrists, shoulders, and hips. Yet her attitude about life was joyful. She felt that she had lived a full life and didn't harbor the resentments I found in myself.

Betty was currently hospitalized for a hip replacement. One of her artificial hips needed to be replaced with a newer model. She was also being treated for kidney problems that had resulted from one of her medications. She had countless stories of the "screwups" that had gone on in her institutional life. But she also was aware of the gifts that her hospital life had bestowed on her. She was especially touched by the people she had met. She felt that this institution, in particular, drew to it some of the most interesting people life had to offer. I felt she was one of the most interesting people *I* had ever met, so her belief had credibility for me. She had a devoted boyfriend who supported her throughout her time in our room.

Once when I returned from a painful procedure, Betty shouted through our curtain divider, "Just you yell it out, Gayle. It helps, and it's good for them to know what you're going through. To hell with being brave. Yell it out. You deserve it." A true veteran of hospitals, supporting me to acknowledge my pain. God had sent me one of His best, and I was grateful.

Remembering Betty's comment about all the interesting people in the hospital made me think back. I was reminded of all the characters I had met during the past year. Once a short, thin, old man with white hair went past my door mumbling something. I could hear him mumbling past other doors, too, as he went down the hall. Then he came back to my door and asked if he could come in. Excited to have my curiosity satisfied, I didn't hesitate to invite him in. He pulled up a chair to my bed and explained his interest in me. When he noticed my name was Gayle and that I had a guitar in my lap, it reminded him of his niece who lived in Kansas. Her name was Gayle, spelled the same way, and she also played the guitar.

I asked him what brought him to the hospital that day. He told me that when he retired, the Lord came to him with a mission. He was instructed to go to all the hospitals in town, walk down the halls, and bless all the rooms. He had been able to work out a schedule that covered three hospitals in a week. At this point it was all he was able to do. Once in a while, when the spirit moved him, he would stop in and chat with a patient.

He asked if he could pick at my guitar. I had never

become adept at the instrument and had hoped that with practice I would improve. It was a pleasure to have someone else play it. He played fun songs like "You Are My Sunshine." He was a bright moment in an otherwise dull day. After he left, a couple of nurses stopped in to ask me what he had said. They had watched him come and go, but he had never stopped to talk to them, and they were curious about him. I shared what I knew and realized that he had been a special gift to me that day.

On another occasion I met a young man who stopped in to tell me his story. He arrived in a wheelchair and shared with me that he was there to have the remainder of his already amputated limb cut off. As he understood it, this procedure would resolve the problems he had been having with his prosthesis. His injury occurred after a night of drinking. He passed out on some railroad tracks, and a passing train severed his leg. He was frightened by the idea of having his leg cut off again.

I asked him if he had changed his drinking habits after the accident. He replied that only two things had changed in his life: his leg and the fact that he stayed away from railroad tracks when he drank. He left me feeling grateful for my sobriety.

Another time I saw an Indian performing a ceremony on the hospital lawn. The story behind this man's behavior was never told to me, but it made me think there were other people in the hospital using alternative healing methods.

As fascinating as it was for me to think back and remember these interesting people, one fact now stood out for me: my life in the hospital was becoming more separate from my life outside. They were like two different worlds. Visitors were scarce now, and Steve was totally immersed in his responsibilities at home. He tried to find ways to support me, but because we weren't connected emotionally, he wasn't successful.

The emotional barrier was illustrated the one night Steve arrived with a surprise for me. He brought me a new winter jacket, made of rough leather and lined in fleece. It was unusual for Steve to bring me a present. I was pleased he had been thinking of me, but I struggled with the kind of jacket he had chosen. It reflected Steve's taste, not mine. My heart felt that it represented how distant we had become. An active, outdoors woman would enjoy the jacket that Steve bought. At this point in my life, I wanted clothing that helped me feel soft and feminine. My resistance to this gift increased when Steve told me he had left Stephanie at home alone sleeping in her crib. He and Sherri had gone out on his motorcycle to pick out the jacket for me.

What had happened to our marriage? It seemed at first that Steve and I had grown closer because of my accident. We started to share our thoughts and feelings, and we became more vulnerable with each other. But after a while, we adjusted to our new roles and the wall between us reappeared. We were both so involved with our separate roles—mine as the patient and his as the single parent—that we didn't want to think about each other's situation. It was too overwhelming. This coat also seemed to say to me, "I want a different woman, not you, not an invalid."

I also had a sick feeling inside about Steve thinking it was O.K. to leave Stephanie alone in the house, just because she was sleeping. I was speechless. A rare moment. My silence wasn't missed by Steve. He got angry that I wasn't thrilled; and I got angry that he had left Stephanie alone. I thanked him for the jacket and asked him never to leave her alone again.

I believe all this emotional turmoil also played itself out on a physical level in my body. After my surgery, complications set in. I had a yeast infection from the I.V. antibiotics, a rash on my buttocks from lying in one position, and a sore on my heel. And to top it off, my I.V.s weren't lasting very long. On February 17 the on-call doctor was requested to come because I needed a new I.V. to be started. He tried for two, maybe three, hours and utilized tourniquets on both arms, hot packs, and other tricks he had learned. He could not find one vein in either arm that would tolerate an I.V. He told me he wanted to insert one in my chest. I told him that I had had that before and that it didn't work.

After a lengthy discussion and after facing the fact that there were no more options open to me, I conceded to the chest I.V. When the doctor was about to do it, I clenched my fist, squinted my face, held my breath, saying, "God is with me, God is with me," in rapid succession.

The doctor tried to encourage me. "Gayle, I can see that you are anxious about this procedure, and I am willing to work with you in getting through this. Listen to what you are saying. The only thing about his procedure that is painful is the initial prick—and if I accidentally go through your bone, which I won't do because I have done this procedure a number of times before. Try to relax. Pay attention to your breathing. Listen to your words."

His promise was consoling. I felt my body begin to relax as I attended to my words and my breathing. I felt the prick of the needle. That was followed by a searing pain as the needle hit my bone. He apologized and told me that he had to continue, that the worst was over. That part was true. The I.V. lasted two days. Then it was determined that oral antibiotics would have to suffice. This meant I could go home.

I was discharged on February 28, with orders to report to the clinic in one week.

[16]

Having a Hoffman fixator on my leg brought me much unwanted attention. When I was out in public, I was constantly asked about my leg. People would come to our restaurant table, stop me in a store, on sidewalks, at the movies, wherever. "What happened to your leg? Does it hurt? Does that go all the way through your leg?"

At first I felt like typing out a statement about my leg and handing it to all those nosy people, but mostly I wanted them not to ask me. When I was out to dinner, the last item I wanted to talk about was my leg. But as much as I hated being asked, I always answered their questions. One of the assignments Sharon gave me was to tell people, "It's none of your business."

I found this assignment nearly impossible to do. One day we all went to Brainerd, a town about three hours northwest of Minneapolis, to visit the Paul Bunyon Recreational Park. Upon entering the park, tourists are greeted by a two-story statue of Paul Bunyon and his ox Blue. This statue not only says "hello" but strikes up conversations with the people coming into the park. When Paul Bunyon saw me coming toward him on crutches, he said, "What happened to your leg?" For the first time I was able to say, "It's none of your business." Steve was watching at the time, and he clapped for me. It was my small beginning in taking care of myself and setting boundaries with people.

The other aspect of the Hoffman fixator that I found troublesome was the care involved. Each of the twelve pin sites had to be cleaned every day. It came to a head one morning while I was doing my daily leg chores. I was overwhelmed with a feeling of being sick and tired of pin cleanings, wound irrigations, and sterile bandage changes. Out of frustration and impatience at the lengthy healing process, I started to cry. I missed the support and encouragement from the nurses I had while in the hospital.

Sherri happened to come by my room and noticed I was crying. She looked at me with her big blue eyes and with the sincerity of a thirty-year-old she said in her five-year-old voice, "How can I help you, Mom?"

I explained to her the procedure for keeping bandages sterile and performing different tasks with which I thought she could assist me. She was able to comprehend it all and became my assist-ant. What a blessing she was, not only as a helper but as a support!

Basically, I did not like the Hoffman fixator because it was so much work and caused such a commotion when I went out. It did free me to walk with crutches, but I found that I still used the wheelchair more than the crutches because of the pain and swelling I experienced when I was on the crutches too long.

The support I was now getting from Sherri didn't make up for empty feelings I was still experiencing in my marriage. They came into sharp focus on Stephanie's second birthday in March, 1980. It was a quiet party with just a few close friends and relatives.

Stephanie wasn't feeling well that day and didn't want to participate much in her party. Steve was aware of Stephanie's disinterest and made an effort playfully to engage her. She looked adorable in her light blue dress, blonde curly hair, and big brown eyes. I also found Steve very appealing. He was lying on the floor with Stephanie, dressed in his flannel plaid shirt, blue jeans, and white socks. He was soft and nurturing with her; his love for her emanated from his being. I thought how lucky she was to be loved so much by him. My heart ached.

A part of me felt jealous of the attention and the relationship that Steve had with the girls. I felt left out and unattractive. Things weren't good between Steve and me. We had started couples counseling with Sharon, but Steve didn't want to continue. Our sex life was practically nonexistent. I purchased some seductive undergarments, thinking they might be helpful. That night I waited for the kids to go to bed and changed into them. It was hard to create an enticing entrance on crutches, but I did the best I could. Steve was reading the paper, pretending I wasn't standing there. When I pressured him into commenting, he said, "Your body is gross. I feel cheated. You don't look at all like you used to. You're full of scars now, and I don't find that attractive."

His words hit deep. I went into the bedroom and looked into the mirror. I saw an incision below my right breast and a smaller scar below that from a gall bladder surgery. There were incisions on each hip and over my left buttock from the bone grafts. My left buttock had a thick red line from inserting the Schneider nail, and my right thigh had two huge patches of scar tissue from the skin graft. Then, of course, I saw my severely deformed left leg with a metal contraption hanging off of it. I was a mess.

Part of me understood that Steve was in the middle of his own process of acceptance, but most of me felt ugly, repulsive, and unlovable. These issues ran deep with me. It was as if my body was displaying all my inside pain. It was a difficult time.

One of the simple pleasures we did still enjoy as a family was going out to visit our land. It was a thirteen-acre lot about thirty miles from town. Steve went out there often and cut wood for our wood stove. He loved being there and hoped one day to sell our house and build on that land. I had mixed feelings about living that far from town, but it seemed like a long-term goal, and I didn't worry about it. Watching the girls help Steve unload wood gave me great pleasure. It also made Steve feel good to go out and cut the wood. Sometimes I would go with him just to get outside. I wasn't much help, but we were all together.

I was still going to clinic every couple of weeks. Occasionally Steve would take me, but usually friends did. By May, Dr. Gustillo said that the tibia had not mended; it was still in two pieces. He suggested I put some pressure on the bone to stimulate it. He ordered my Hoffman fixator to be taken off and a full-length walking cast to be put on. I was to use crutches while bearing a little weight on my left leg. I hadn't done that in a year.

A cast presented its own set of problems. With little feeling in my leg, I would get pressure sores and not know it. These sores were susceptible to infection and required the same care as my other open wounds. A window would be cut out of the cast to expose any open wounds I had so that I could still clean them daily. Because the cast went from my toes to the very top of my leg, baths were out and sponge baths were in. Yuk! But now my leg looked more normal, and most people didn't ask about it. What I liked best about a cast was that it made me feel like anybody else with a broken leg. And with the cast, I no longer needed the wheelchair. It was a strange feeling to see it go because a part of me liked the security that came with it. It was a little scary to be on my own again.

Steve purchased a car for me from a friend. The body was rusted out, so he and his dad fixed it and painted it. It was a small car, and I didn't think I could get into the driver's seat with my full-length cast. One day, with the encouragement of a friend, I crutch-walked out to the car and found that I did fit into the front seat. A wonderful sense of freedom filled my being as I came to realize I could again drive a car. It had been over a year. Steve was nervous about it, but there was no holding me back now.

School started for me in June, 1980. I had been accepted into the chemical dependency program at St. Mary's Junior College, a certificate program for people who wanted to counsel the chemically dependent. Steve recognized that I needed to do something more with my life, but he made it clear that he didn't like my going back to school. He never discussed it with me. When he was a child, he had found school to be a negative experience. I assumed that was why he didn't want to talk about it. One night he shared a fear: I would meet an intellectual man at school and run off with him. It surprised me at this point that Steve would even care if I left.

It had been almost ten years since I had last attended school. I had gone to a state college for a year shortly after high school. I had intended to transfer to a school out west when Steve asked me to marry him. I had decided to become Steve's wife and let go of my scholastic ambitions. Now I was nervous about competing with other adults. Doubts about my abilities preoccupied my mind. I was grateful that the grading system was set up in a way that a student never had to see grades unless there was the desire to do so. I never looked at mine; I thought it might discourage me. Many years later, when I needed a transcript from this program, I found out I had received almost straight A's.

I liked the program immediately. It challenged me intellectually and the material stimulated introspection, which I also liked. I felt free at school to be Gayle. I wasn't a patient, a wife, or a mother when I was at school. No one here needed anything from me. I could bathe in the pursuit of knowledge and relish in conversation with like minds. I found it exhilarating. Also it was wonderful to be productive again. People hardly ever talked about my leg. Discussions were mostly focused on the different projects in which we were involved.

A fellow student named Ben and I became sounding boards for each other. We were both in unsatisfactory relationships. We did a lot of complaining and comparing notes. This helped me acknowledge that my needs weren't getting met in my relationship with Steve, but it didn't help me define other ways they might be met.

In July, Steve and I went to court about my leg. Until now, all I had been told about the case was that the driver and his mother, who was a passenger, denied hitting me. Steve's lawyer, David, suspected their denial was an attempt to protect the family fortune.

We drove to Brainerd with three other bikers and got rooms in the same motel. The bikers had come along to testify at the pending trial. Every one except me went swimming to help lessen the tension; I stayed in the room because of my full- length cast. One of the bikers asked if I would like to come and just watch. It felt good to be asked by someone, but I couldn't bear to watch Steve being playful with other women. He had been especially attentive to the one woman biker who was with us, and she was charmed by his interest. Jealousy penetrated my being, and I felt my scars and inadequacies overcoming me. While everyone was gone, I had a good cry.

We went to the courthouse and waited outside the courtroom while Steve's lawyer met with the defendants' lawyer. Soon David came out and said, "There is no money as far as I can tell from my investigation. They would like to settle for the policy limit, which is $50,000 and a personal check for $7,000. Is that O.K. with you?"

I was totally confused. I had no information on which to base a decision; and yet, I was being asked to make one. Up to this point, Steve had kept all this business between David and himself. Steve prodded me, "Say it's O.K."

I got mad and exclaimed, "I don't get it, why $7,000? And why did you think earlier there was money here if now there obviously isn't?"

Nobody wanted an argument; they just wanted to settle. So my questions weren't answered, and the settlement was made. I wished I hadn't even gone. What I found out later was that David took the customary legal fee—one-third of the insurance payment—and all I could see he had done was to investigate if the farmer had hidden money. So we ended up with $35,000 dollars and a promise for a check for $7,000 to come later.

Thirty-five thousand dollars wasn't much money in my mind. There were unanswered questions and a feeling in my stomach of being tricked. The damage to my leg, my pain and suffering, Steve's loss of a career in tower cranes, day-care costs, hospital bills, and the loss my children suffered from my absence—these things couldn't have been compensated by any amount of money. But to receive only $35,000 was ridiculous. David told us it was common practice, after a low settlement in a personal injury case, to negotiate hospital bills down, and he recommended refraining from paying them at this time. So instead of paying hospital bills, I spent the money on enjoyable things. Years later these bills surfaced in my life and demanded payment.

First, Steve and I decided to remodel the house. We

took out a low-income loan for part of the funds and used some of my settlement money. Then I gave Steve $6,000 to buy himself a brand-new Harley Davidson dresser—the cadillac of motorcycles. It came with a windshield, comfortable seats, side boxes for carrying gear, and a wind protector. For me, the settlement money paid for a much-awaited trip to Virginia Beach, as soon as I had a break in school. Virginia Beach was the headquarters city for the organization that sponsored my prayer and meditation group. It represented a spiritual oasis to me. The bike and the trip were fantasies Steve and I had told each other about at a time when we never thought they would manifest. At this time Steve had little enthusiasm for my fantasy. A portion of the money was put away into savings, some bills were paid, and the remainder was spent on assorted presents.

When the remodeling started on the house, Stephanie's asthma developed dramatically. I became familiar with emergency rooms in the middle of the night. Steve was working long hours, so I was usually the one to take her. It turned out that if her wheezing had not progressed far enough when we got to the hospital, we would be sent home, only to return a few hours later.

My anxiety grew around her illness. I would start to feel the tension with her first cough. As the asthma attack intensified, I tried to time our visit to the emergency room appropriately so that we wouldn't have to go twice. It didn't take long for me to become totally unreasonable whenever Stephanie's asthma was evident.

One night Steve decided to stay up with her. He was determined to show me how it should be done. I was so relieved to have a break that I fell asleep, only to awaken about midnight with Steve cursing the doctors for sending him home without treating Stephanie. I could relate. It made a person feel stupid, not to mention the wasted energy.

This was a time in Stephanie's life when consistent care from a single doctor would have helped a lot. But unfortunately, Stephanie's previous physician had left General, and now she usually was treated in the emergency room by a series of overworked and very tired doctors. Her illness was a constant strain on the whole family, and it seemed to be getting worse.

Meanwhile, my doctors were discouraged by the lack of mending in my tibia. They decided again that I needed to put more pressure on it to stimulate the bone growth. A full leg brace was ordered, to replace the cast. The brace consisted of two leather straps that laced up the front of my lower leg and thigh. The two metal braces on each side of these straps kept my leg stiff, forcing my hip to take most of the pressure when I walked. A hinge at the knee could be released when I sat down, so my leg wouldn't stick out. Finally the brace was attached to an orthopedic shoe.

I was glad to have the cast off, but it didn't take long to learn to hate the brace. It seemed to take forever to put on, and it was cumbersome when I moved. I couldn't simply jump out of bed and do something, unless I hopped. Of course, hopping is exactly what I did most of the time, but it wasn't safe. I still had the option to use my crutches, but my opinion of them had also bottomed-out.

The one blessing that came with this leg brace was the ability to walk longer distances and carry items in my hands. It made traveling much more manageable to me. It seemed like a good time for the vacation to Virginia Beach I had been planning.

[17]

During August, 1980, I traveled to Virginia Beach to visit the headquarters of the Association for Research and Enlightenment, located across the street from the ocean. The A.R.E., which sponsored the prayer and meditation study group I had attended since 1976, was founded in 1931 by Edgar Cayce, a man who helped thousands of people by giving them psychic readings. A library had been established to house his readings and other similar resources. Many of those readings were health related, and the headquarters operation included a Health Services Department that offered some of the treatments referred to by Cayce.

Since I had joined an A.R.E. study group, I had heard about others' adventures at Virginia Beach, and I wanted to experience this magical place myself. During the summer, their week-long seminars on various subjects attracted people from all over the world. It sounded like a great place to meet like-minded, interesting people and learn some new things. My friend Marie decided to come with me.

Steve was so negative about my going on this trip that he didn't even wake up to see me off. Marie's fiancé gave us a lift to the airport. Once I was on the plane, it was as if Steve, hospitals, and responsibilities were a million miles away. I felt as if I could breathe again. I tried to explain the surge of freedom to Marie. "I feel as if I can do anything I want to and nobody will ever know. I could even have an affair and who would care."

Marie was to be married soon after we returned, and she was not receptive to my example. She was going to Virginia Beach for her own reasons, and she did not share my enthusiasm for this personal freedom.

Our accommodations in the Marshalls Motel were right on the oceanfront. We could hear and see the surf from our door. The weather was perfect and the lectures were fascinating. On the beach I constantly encountered interesting people. I met a lawyer who told me about one of his cases. His client from Alaska had been mauled by a polar bear over a period of three days. While in the hospital recovering from her multiple wounds, she discovered she was pregnant. Despite her doctor's warnings, she decided to have her baby and just recently gave birth to a healthy child.

On another occasion, I was enjoying a book as I sat at a table with an umbrella. I noticed a man approaching me. He was about sixty and wore bermuda shorts with a loud print. His white hair and round belly completed the image I formed in my mind: surely this was a nosy tourist who was going to ask about my leg. I tried to appear unapproachable but he came right up to me and said, "When you aren't busy, I have something I'd like to tell you."

I concluded that this man wouldn't take a hint and replied, "I'm not busy. You can talk to me now."

He said, "I want to tell you a story about a small drop of salty water that lived in the ocean. He had lived there all his life, and Little Drop liked it there, surrounded by all his friends.

"One day the sun came out and pulled Little Drop out of the ocean and into the sky. He became saltless as he rose. When Little Drop stopped moving, he became aware of how frightened he was. At first, he thought he was all alone. Then he saw there were other drops of saltless water all around. He heard them talk about how scared they were, too, and how they missed being salty. Somehow this made him feel better."

I thought this man's story was great. I was entranced by him. I wondered why he had chosen to tell it to me. How could he have known how applicable it was to my recent experience?

He continued. "It was cold where they were, so they decided to huddle together and try to warm each other. Soon there were so many drops crowded together, a cloud was formed. It felt better now, less scary. But all of a sudden Little Drop was squeezed out of the cloud and fell to the earth. It hurt when he hit the hard ground.

"Many of the drops had fallen with him. As they gathered together to share their experiences, they formed a small stream which started flowing down a hill. Little Drop cried out, 'Where am I going now?' He soon found himself falling into a storm sewer pipe that was dark and smelly. Time seemed to last forever.

"Little Drop eventually flowed through a series of pipes that led into a water heater. It was so hot in there that Little Drop thought he would disappear. Then he found himself again in a series of pipes that quickly brought him back into the light as he landed in a sink full of dirty dishes. He felt soapy, lost, and tired of new sensations.

"After a while he was sucked down a drain and back into a pipe. He felt himself begin to cool down. In time, light appeared again, and Little Drop found himself outside in a stream with many other drops. It smelled good there. As they joined with other drops they formed a river. Days passed and he flowed with the river, learning all about river life.

"Then one day he felt an intense, burning sensation wash through his body. It hurt and it felt familiar. He realized he was back in the ocean again, and he was salty. It felt good to be home. He wasn't the same Little Drop that had left the ocean long ago. He was salty again but he was different."

I was spellbound by the fable and didn't know what to say. Then the man told me I was like the little drop. In the future I would be like I used to be, only different. He continued, "And one day you'll be walking down the street, and a man will whistle at your beautiful legs. You will smile knowing everything that was behind that whistle."

His story filled me with hope. I remembered my bargain with God—a total healing plus a life of service. I felt affirmed that I would heal and have my life back again, even though it would be different. I asked this man what he did for a living. He said he was a retired minister. What a joy to have been his total congregation that day!

Another day Marie and I went to the cypress gardens—a state park with a swamp, lush with vegetation, and cypress trees. With my leg brace, I wondered how long I would last on the trails. I had heard that the water was pure and the area was magical. The air felt full of energy, and the swamp seemed to stir with excitement as we entered. My body felt light, and it was easy for me to walk. We hiked two miles that day. Before that day I had been able to accomplish only about two blocks.

One of the most significant parts of my week in Virginia Beach was the friendship I struck up with Carolyn, a past-life regressionist. We met on the beach, and it felt easy to be together. We chatted about life and how it had unfolded for both of us. I wanted to know more about what she did, so I had a regression by her later in the week. I found it to be a fascinating process.

Carolyn arranged equipment to tape our session so I could review it later. She had me lie down on a couch, then led me through several mental exercises. They required me to imagine myself first shorter, then taller, and finally lighter. Next her suggestions asked me to imagine myself floating up away from the earth. After a while I was told to land back on the earth. When I landed, she asked me to imagine looking down at my feet and to describe what I saw. Next I was to describe my clothes and my surroundings. It was a surprise to see that I was wearing something from a different era. Apparently I was connecting with a past-life experience.

Carolyn guided me to see in my imagination several key things: one important moment in that lifetime; the time of my death; and the period right after my death, in order to review and to see if I had accomplished my goals or left any unfinished business.

We visited three different lifetimes using this technique. One was a life with Steve in the Old West. We were pioneers, and he had taken me out to an isolated prairie home. He was an alcoholic and had eventually abandoned me there with our children.

After the regression was over, we reviewed this lifetime. Carolyn pointed out both similarities and differences in my experience with Steve now: both of us struggling with alcoholism and recovery, my insistence at the time of the accident that he commit to stay with the children, and his decision to stay and take full responsibility for the home front. Carolyn indicated that the current lifetime was an opportunity to heal old wounds between us.

Special one-to-one encounters such as those with Carolyn and the storytelling minister were a very important part of my week. But so were my times at A.R.E. headquarters. As a conferee, I could utilize the physical therapies offered through the Health Services Department. The two therapies I tried during this conference were a colonic and a massage. The colonic, which was performed by a registered nurse, is similar to an enema except that it is more intense. It cleanses the entire colon, and I thought it would help rid my body of traces of the drugs from my hospitalization. The massage therapist had been trained by Doctor Reilly, a contemporary of Edgar Cayce's, who followed the suggestions in the readings. Reilly had developed a specialized massage technique, and I hoped it would assist the circulation in my leg.

My massage therapist also did some range-of-motion exercises with my body. I started to explain to her that since my last bone graft I hadn't been able to loosen up my left hip. Suddenly I realized my hip was free from any stiffness. Tears came to my eyes as I became conscious of the miracle that had just happened to my hip. I asked her how she did it, and she explained that she was a healer. As I looked up at her angelic face, she continued to tell me her story.

Once an injury had severely scarred her face. But she experienced a miraculous healing, and since that time the gift had been passed to her for sharing with others. The story was a little hard to believe because her face was flawless in my eyes—not a trace of scar tissue. "Beauty is in the eye of the beholder," she responded to my doubt.

At night people gathered in the lounge of the motel—the Oceanscope Room—to listen to music and discuss the day's events. The Marshalls Motel was across the street from the A.R.E., and it was the lodging that was used by most A.R.E. conferees. The Oceanscope Room was a community gathering place with large windows facing directly onto the beach.

One night a man named Dan played his guitar. As I listened, I became aware of an attraction between us. Later that evening I met Dan on the beach. We sat on the sand and both became totally absorbed in our conversation. Eventually we kissed. He held me and touched my heart in a way I had never before experienced. It was sexual, but it was also nurturing. I finally told him I was married, and I couldn't continue kissing him. He said he understood and asked if we could just hold each other and keep talking. This was my fantasy coming true: a man who wanted to hold me and who liked to talk. We spent the night on the beach doing just that. My heart felt comforted.

In the morning I went to get Marie to see if she wanted to join us for breakfast. She was livid. She was Steve's friend, too, and couldn't understand what was happening here. I was not sure what was happening, but it felt wonderful. Leaving Marie behind, we had breakfast in town and enjoyed our remaining moments together.

Later that day I found Carolyn on the beach and talked to her about my experiences with Dan. She told me the energy in Virginia Beach was strong and it often accelerated the growth process. Many people who come are needy for kindred souls, and their hearts respond to the intensity of the energy. Sometimes this results in people becoming strongly attracted. According to Carolyn, the heart center opens and can be more receptive to a higher love. She thought perhaps there was a lesson to be learned: maybe Dan was a former companion, someone I had been with in a past life, and we had renewed the connection at a time when I needed reassurance as a woman.

What I experienced from Carolyn was acceptance. There was no judgment in what she said to me. It was very helpful because usually I am my harshest judge. In fact, I was surprised that I wasn't all over my case. Dan and I saw each other for brief periods during my last forty-eight hours in Virginia Beach. I realized that what Dan experienced and what I experienced were different. I wrote him a letter and told him about the love that I felt when I was with him. My plan was for him to read it after I left. But he got it early and managed to corner me before my departure. He told me he was sorry if he had hurt me. He cared for me, but it was not love. I was so enchanted with him I could barely hear his words.

[18]

Coming home, I was left to my own thoughts as Marie stared at me with accusing eyes. I wondered how I would handle being with Steve. Keeping it a secret was not an option, and I doubted that he would believe that we had not been sexual. Steve arrived home a few hours after me. He came in, sat beside me, looked me straight in the eye, and said, "Tell me about your trip."

This was very strange. He never wanted to hear what I did. I told him that Virginia Beach was wonderful and I would like to go back. While I was there, I met a man whom I felt very close to, but he did not share my feelings. Although we had spent some time together alone, we had not been sexual. Steve believed me, and he calmly told me that he had known something had happened. He could feel it.

As the days passed, I fantasized about Dan, reliving our time together over and over in my mind. I wrote him and he wrote back. Terrified that Steve would see the letters, I was sure to get the mail before he came home.

Finally, one day when I was doing dishes, Steve blurted out angrily, "That's it. You make a decision. Either you live here with me or you go to Virginia and live there with him. But I want him out of my house, as of now."

He was right, and I could hear that he had had enough of my daydreaming. How silly of me to think that I could be with Dan in my head and that Steve wouldn't notice. I knew that Dan did not reciprocate my feeling and that underneath it all what I wanted most was Steve. So I made a conscious decision to release Dan and try to stay present with Steve. After the decision was made, the work started. It took a long time to accomplish my goal. My friends were patient as I repeatedly spoke of struggles to release my fantasies about Dan. I also had to make the decision to stay present with Steve over and over again. But something was different at home and it helped this process. Steve was attempting to win my affections. Somehow my relationship with Dan had made me more appealing to Steve.

It was hard to trust Steve's renewed interest. In fact, it took me a while even to see it. But it felt wonderful. He was flirting with me, teasing me, and desiring me. My body had all of a sudden become attractive to him again. He asked me out on dates and started sharing his thoughts. He told me about his days at work, the struggles he encountered, and the accomplishments he was making. Sometimes, he even asked me about school. I didn't think he was truly interested, but it showed me that he was making an effort. The twinkle in his eye was there again when he looked at me. I felt as if I had recaptured his attention.

We became partners once more: planning together the things we wanted to accomplish, running the household, parenting, and paying the bills. We discussed the possibility of my working part-time as a chemical dependency counselor. It would help alleviate the financial burden he felt. Steve shared his desire to learn more about organic gardening and to start a garden out on the land. He related a story he had heard about a technique to keep certain bugs off the plants.

"You sprinkle flour on the leaves, and when the bugs walk across the leaf, it sticks to their little legs. It doesn't take long for it to build up on their legs. The weight of the flour disables them, and they fall off the leaf."

At night Steve would start a fire in the fireplace and ask me to enjoy it with him. We also made a point of dating more, going out for dinner or seeing a movie. One time when we were out with a group of his friends, I watched with envy how one couple seemed to be so connected. I said to Steve, "I wish you would be more like your friend."

Steve was interested in what I meant by that, and I explained that I wished he would touch me more often in public, hold my hand, or give me a spontaneous hug. He smiled and responded immediately. He cared enough to hear my need. That touched my heart and healed another wound from the past. I could feel my love for Steve growing again.

On September 4, 1980, I had a dream that immediately seemed very significant. I called it "Earth Changes." In the dream I realized that cataclysmic earthquakes and floods—so-called earth changes—had happened during the night. I was in the bedroom of my childhood home and noticed there was an ocean outside my window. Growing up in Minnesota, an ocean obviously wouldn't be expected outside a bedroom window. As the dream continued to unfold, I saw other events that would occur as a result of these earth changes. Several of my friends wouldn't understand what was happening, the relationship with my mother would be disconnected, and Steve would leave this plane of existence, assuring me that we would be reunited at another time.

Gayle and Steve on their way to the lake, July 1971.

Wedding day, February 26, 1972.

Left: *Steve's International tractor, 1973.*

Below: *Steve and Sherri, summer 1976.*

Below: *Steve's 1948 Harley Davidson motorcycle.*

Left: *Gayle's first time outside the hospital since her Memorial Day accident, 1979.*

Left: *Steve's new 1980 Harley Davidson motorcycle.*

Right: *Steve on a bike trip with the X-Winos, 1980.*

Stephanie's second birthday party, March 22, 1980. Gayle is in a wheelchair with a Hoffman fixator on her leg.

Steve with Stephanie at her second birthday party.

Sherri and Stephanie at the last Christmas before Steve's death, 1980.

Gayle's second trip to Virginia Beach, 1981, outside the Marshalls Motel across from the A.R.E. She is wearing a small, white, plastic brace.

Sturgis, South Dakota, motorcycle rally, August 1981.

Stephanie and Sherri at Virginia Beach, November 1982.

Left: *The family back in Minnesota again, December 1983.*

Below: *Steve's friend Pat, who became a strong support for Gayle following Steve's death.*

Right: *Doc, a friend who took Gayle shopping for Sherri's school supplies shortly after Steve's death.*

Doc and Pat.

Sherri, Gayle, and Stephanie in 1992.

[19]

On September 13, I followed Steve to Marie's wedding reception. He rode his bike, and I drove my car. All the way out there, I was preoccupied with the thought of Steve dying. Ever since my dream, I had a strong feeling that Steve was going to die in a motorcycle accident. As I followed him, I thought, "If he crashed, I might run over him with the car." The thought of my being responsible for Steve's death was agonizing. We finally arrived at the reception safely.

It turned out to be a nice evening. Steve asked me to dance. I told him it was nice to be asked, but I didn't think I could dance with my leg brace on. He took me out to the dance floor and had me stand on his feet. We danced in this intimate fashion, and I felt very special.

I found that I was constantly thinking about Steve dying. One day he took me around the house and showed me what I should know in case something happened to him. He did not know about my dream, and his actions indicated to me that he was unconsciously creating closure. By the end of September, I had one of my loud discussions with God. I said, "Don't just tell me Steve's going to die and not give me any time frame. If this is a long-term thing, I need to know. Please give me some sign that will help me keep this in perspective."

The next morning I was awakened by a voice that said clearly, "When Stephanie is four, she will no longer have a daddy." Stephanie would not be four until March of 1982. That was a year and a half away. I felt relieved that I had time and terrified that my fearful thoughts were being confirmed.

Steve and I went out to dinner on September 28 to celebrate his thirtieth birthday. Just before we left, his friend Bob called and asked him to stop by so he could see something on Bob's bike. We had a nice Mexican dinner and then stopped at Bob's. When we drove up, we saw Bob outside in the dark working on his bike under a spotlight. Steve said, "Boy, that Bob is sure getting fanatical about his bike. Look what he's rigged up just to keep working." We got out and watched Bob tinkering with the bike. Then he asked Steve to get him a tool that was lying on his dining room table. When Steve opened the door to the dining room, a bunch of people yelled "SURPRISE!"

Bob and I had planned together this surprise party for Steve. He was overwhelmed with its thoughtfulness and the number of people who had come to celebrate his birthday. After a while he realized I had instigated the whole thing and that I had successfully lied to him in order to pull it off. He told me later it scared him that he hadn't been able to tell I was lying. I replied that the only reason I could lie so successfully to him was that I knew he would find out the truth in a short time.

Through the next few months, Steve and I grew closer. We explored new levels of intimacy. Trust was re-established, and we started behaving more like new-lyweds. He started to open to some of my interests, and I became more open to his motorcycle friends. We brought in the New Year with a party at our house. Steve invited all his motorcycle friends, and we had our first sober bash. It was a lot of fun.

In January 1981, I joined the European Health Spa to work on learning to walk again. I walked back and forth in the pool without my brace, trying to minimize my limp. It took many months to accomplish the gait I desired.

I told Steve I wanted to go to California to visit my friend Joanne. He said he would like to go with me. In fact, he said he thought the whole family should go, and we would make it into a family vacation. This was not what I had in mind, but I was receptive to the idea when I thought this might be the last chance we would ever have for a family vacation. Steve bought a camper top for the back of his pick-up truck, and he built a bed to go inside it. I made curtains for the windows. Steve envisioned us camping under the stars on our way to and from California.

We went in February. We drove straight through to get there. I saw Joanne for only one night. Both the kids got colds. Stephanie couldn't breathe in the mountains. It rained the day we went to Disneyland. On the way home we were able to camp under the stars in the desert, but the fulfillment of Steve's camping vision was hampered by Spike who rolled in feces. We had no water to clean him. Surprisingly, Steve and I kept our sense of humor, and despite all the problems we were still a functional group when we returned. What helped me keep a positive perspective throughout the trip was my sense that Steve might not be around to do it again.

On the trip Steve told me that he'd noticed my frequent, sarcastic remarks to Sherri. He asked me to lighten up on her and to give her credit for her differences instead of teasing her about them. It seemed odd for Steve to be making these statements. It was certainly a valid concern, and I was grateful he had spoken up. But in the past, he had never expressed opinions about my relationship with the girls.

By March I had put away all my thoughts about Steve dying. Then one night I had a dream that renewed my fears. I was with two little girls watching a tree come down on a house. The whole house crumbled down. We knew the little girls' daddy was inside.

On March 22 we celebrated Stephanie's third birthday with a puppet show. Many of the bikers arrived to support Steve in this celebration. It seemed strange to me that they came to Stephanie's party, but Steve liked it. In the past I would have confronted him on this. I would have pointed out that, in my opinion, it was inappropriate to have his friends come to his daughter's party. But the healing that had taken place in our relationship freed me to be more flexible and tolerant of our differences.

On April 6 Dr. Gustillo asked me to come back as an inpatient and have the Schneider nail in my femur removed. I remembered one of my roommates having this procedure done. She was out within two days and ate a hamburger after surgery. I checked this out with Dr. Gustillo, and he concurred that it would take three days at the most. I was admitted back into the hospital on May 18.

My new doctors introduced themselves one at a time, and I soon found out that they expected me to stay three weeks for I.V. antibiotic treatment. They acted as if I should have expected this because of my history of osteomyelitis. I insisted that Dr. Gustillo be notified and found that he was out of town for three days. Before surgery I tried to contact the anesthesiologist to discuss my problems with post-operative nausea. I was told that he was a busy man and usually saw patients only in the operating room.

After surgery I refused I.V. antibiotics and tried to explain that I had no veins left. My refusal led to a requirement that I sign a waiver protecting the hospital from any repercussions from my actions. On my medical chart, one of my doctors wrote that I was a disagreeable, unreasonable, and hostile patient. It was the worst relationship I had experienced with a doctor.

Finally Dr. Gustillo responded to the situation, and I was released on May 21. Before I left, I was given two new apparatuses: a splint that came to my knee and a Bassett electromagnetic stimulator. The splint was great because it was easy to put on (no more laces) and easy to fit over clothes. The stimulator was to be worn on the leg for ten hours a day. It was supposed to stimulate bone growth.

Steve took me home and surprised me with a sign on the house that read, "Welcome Home, Mom." It was another one of those times when I was happy and frustrated simultaneously. The sign was nice, but Steve had used a good sheet and had sprayed it with black paint in the kitchen. There was black overspray on various cupboard doors. This time, however, the effort and the thoughtfulness of the sign and the warm welcome were more important to me than a sheet and some black paint on my cupboards. I didn't say anything except, "Thanks, it's great to be home."

I made a decision never again to return to clinic or the hospital. This last hospital experience was the final straw. It had left me keenly aware of the bitterness I had stored during the past two years. Also the warmth I was receiving at home was too precious to leave again. I was tired of being in the hands of strangers— tired of being poked, cut, and treated with disrespect. I wanted my life back again. Somehow I would manage without returning.

Late May was the time for the annual X-Wino Turkey Roast. The previous year Steve had gone out and helped cook the turkeys. But this year he wanted to include me. I rode out there with him on his motorcycle. It was scary, but I had to do it for Steve. Somehow it symbolized my renewed trust in him and my desire to share in his life again. It was a great party with good food and games. At one point I felt a little abandoned by Steve because he was so involved with the activities; but he noticed that I was unhappy and took the time to check it out with me. He apologized and made a point to include me more often. This sensitive, caring behavior was an incredibly new and wonderful part of Steve. I totally enjoyed it.

At the campfire that night, Steve was given a broomball signed by all the team players, and he was asked to be the new captain. Broomball is a sport similar to hockey. Instead of skates, hockey sticks, and pucks, broomball players use tennis shoes with little suction cups, stiff brooms, and a soccer ball. The winter before he joined the team, Steve discovered it to be a fun winter activity.

At the campfire he was also given a three-year medallion from his sponsor. It celebrated three years of continuous sobriety. Then, to my surprise, he asked me to stand up and gave me his medallion to celebrate my three years of sobriety. I felt very much in love with this new Steve who was continually surprising me with his ability to show his love for me.

The first of June, I went with my friend Donna to Virginia Beach for the second time. Although I was still meeting regularly with my group in Minnesota, my main motivation for returning to the A.R.E. headquarters was the incredible healing energy my soul felt there. It was hard to know exactly what made it that kind of experience for me—the people, the air, the ocean, the available services, or the philosophical support I felt. I had not been seeing Beth lately for healings because I was trying to forget about my leg. So I knew it was not physical needs that enticed me to return. I couldn't be totally sure how much my experiences with Dan had colored my first visit to Virginia Beach, but I suspected that my yearning to return ran much deeper than that.

This time Steve got up to see me off and was supportive of my going. He even took a picture of us as we drove off to the airport. Before I left, Dan was mentioned only once. I brought it up, telling Steve it was all ancient history.

Virginia Beach was as wonderful as I had remembered it. The day after our arrival, I ran into Dan on the beach. He told me he was running late and that he was on his way home to have lunch with his new wife. It was unexpected news and it hurt. In contrast, I had a wonderful reunion with Carolyn. I had kept in touch with her, and it was great to see her again. We have remained friends ever since. Even though my main motivation for the trip wasn't to heal my body, nevertheless, I decided to utilize the Health Services Department again, and I had another colonic and massage.

I met a lady named Jo on the beach one day. She told me about her work with castor oil packs. I had read about them; they were a remedy often referred to in the Cayce readings for a variety of ailments. The packs consisted of a double layer of cloth soaked in castor oil and usually placed on the abdomen with heat for about an hour. Jo explained her work with what she called "castor oil beds." She wrapped people in sheets soaked in castor oil and let them sleep all night like that. She performed this on her patients for three or four nights in a row, then stopped for three or four nights. Repeating this treatment over an extended period of time, she had seen significant healing in people with paralysis and even in some comatose victims. She suggested I try it with my leg as soon as I felt done with traditional medical procedures.

I thought to myself, "I *am* done with the medical procedures." But I was in denial concerning my leg and its needs. That kept me from pursuing Jo's technique for several months.

When it came time to return home, I reflected on the

impact this magical place had on me. My heart felt like dancing and my faith felt renewed. As much as my love for Steve had grown, I grieved leaving the beach and returning to my life in Minnesota. This time I left Dan in Virginia Beach with his new wife. The fantasies were gone.

Steve welcomed me warmly and asked sincerely about my trip. I stated that I loved it there, Dan was married, and I wasn't attracted to him any more. I also told Steve that I loved him very much. Steve confessed that while I was gone he had received two separate offers from women. I asked him if he had been tempted. He admitted he had, but said he realized that he had everything he wanted at home.

This led to a great discussion about our marriage. We both acknowledged that it was a marriage between two very different people. We both admitted having considered divorce at different points. Neither of us wanted that now, but we did talk about ways to find more freedom in this marriage, and alternative living situations were explored. We recognized the times our basic differences caused us the most difficulty: when we were socializing or playing together. In order to deal partially with this, we decided we should take separate vacations. He would do his biking and I would do my spiritual quests. We also declared our love and commitment to each other and our children. Our parenting was a place we could come together. This was the most adult-like discussion we had ever had. I was impressed with how our relationship had matured and how much safer I felt in it.

My return from Virginia Beach also marked my first internship at St. Mary's Rehabilitation Center. My assignment was for three months as a chemical dependency counselor-intern. My mentor was a wonderful lady named Mary Ellen. One of the first items I confronted with this position was the amount of walking it entailed—up and down long halls and stairs. My leg was not supported enough for all this activity, and my pain level went up a notch.

I also found it difficult to feel like a staff member because I empathized so strongly with the clients. I had gotten sober myself three years earlier in this same program. Mary Ellen helped me process through my role confusion and, as my three months progressed, my professional image started to emerge. I discovered I had good insight, and my direct manner was a helpful tool in dealing with a disease that involves strong denial. I also learned that I was uncomfortable discussing sexuality issues and that I tended to lose my power around aggressive clients. One time when I was explaining something to my group, using the blackboard to emphasize my point, a client took the chalk from my hand and completed my lecture from his perspective. I found this so threatening that I didn't even confront his behavior. Fortunately the group ended soon.

St. Mary's was a great place to learn, and I felt my confidence growing under Mary Ellen's guidance. But I was grateful that before graduation I had an additional internship requirement in another, unfamiliar setting.

One day at work, a staff nurse said that I should see a doctor about my leg. I appeared in pain when I walked and he suspected an infection. I ignored this comment and continued to deny any pain or problems with my leg.

Since spring Steve had gone on many weekend bike trips. My dreams continued to warn of Steve's death in a motorcycle accident. I grieved for him while he went on those weekend trips, waiting for the phone call that would tell me he had been in an accident. In the early morning of July 4, another dream about Steve was just starting when I forced myself to awaken and told myself, "No more, no more dreams about Steve."

In July he started staying home more often. He suggested that we go on some weekend camping trips. It wasn't my favorite thing to do, but Steve made it sound appealing enough that I consented. The last weekend of July we went to Banning Junction, about ninety miles away. It was our second family camping trip since Steve had developed this idea. The girls loved camping, and Steve was definitely in his element in the woods. He would set up the tent, do all the cooking, and go for walks with the kids. On this particular trip we all felt very connected. When we came home, I shared at my AA meeting that this was the first time, in the nine-and-a-half years of marriage, that I felt happy to be married.

August brought a yearly bike rally at Sturgis, South Dakota. Ten years earlier Steve had started there but his bike broke down. Since then, he had tried unsuccessfully to return there and participate in the bike rally. This year he planned to go with his friend Pat. At the last minute Pat decided not to go. Steve went anyway by himself.

I got off work at St. Mary's early that day to catch him and say good-bye before he left. When I got home, I found a note: "We got off work at 2:30, so I'm leaving early. Love you all very much, and already I'm missing ya. All my love, Steve." Another sign of how things had changed. Steve never left notes unless I specifically asked him to.

The next night, on August 8, I got the dreaded call. "Mrs. Martinez, I am a doctor calling you from Pierre, South Dakota. I am sorry to inform you that your husband has been in a serious motorcycle accident."

[20]

The doctor on the phone said that Steve had a head injury, but they had no way of knowing at this point how serious it was. He recommended that Steve be transferred to Minneapolis right away because some head injuries swell soon after the accident. If Steve's tissue started to swell, he could not be moved because it would aggravate the problem.

I felt sick in the pit of my stomach and panic in my chest. My brain turned to mush and all I could think of were my dreams. I understood only that the doctor needed my permission to fly Steve home, and I gave it.

My friend Anita had been staying overnight. She was a member of my study group and knew about my dreams. While she held me, I cried, unable to rid myself of the panic I felt. I tried to think of what Steve would want me to do. In response I called his lawyer David, his sister, and Pat, the biker with whom he had planned this trip.

Pat met me at the hospital, and I asked him to take responsibility for informing all the bikers about what was happening. As we waited for Steve to arrive, I started smoking again, after having successfully quit for three months. Netty, the nurses' assistant who came to give me hugs when I was a patient, came by and expressed her concern for Steve. When he finally did arrive at the hospital several hours later, I was away getting something to drink. Before I was allowed to see him, there was another long wait while he was examined and treated. I walked into Intensive Care and saw him lying on the bed. His head was shaved, there was a tube in his nose, and he was attached to a respirator. A bolt in his head was attached to a monitor, recording brain activity. I started to cry. I hardly recognized the strong, healthy man with whom I had just gone camping. Terror consumed my body, causing me to feel lightheaded and shakey. My heart felt as if it were exploding with pain.

It was explained to me that Steve had hit an unmarked ridge in the road, while trying to pass a car. He had flown off his motorcycle and landed on his head. His head injury was severe, but they did not know the extent of the damage. He had been placed in a barbiturate coma to keep his brain from any excess stimulation. Its swelling was a natural response to the head injury, but stimulation would increase the problem. Usually this swelling process lasted three days. When it subsided, they would be able to assess better the extent of the damage.

When I was finally alone with Steve, I stood by his bed and closed my eyes. I spoke to his spirit, acknowledging how much I loved him. I could feel Steve behind me. He wrapped his arms around me and whispered, "I love you." I could feel his presence. Suddenly I remembered that I was in I.C.U. and opened my eyes, losing the moment.

I stayed with Steve as much as possible during the next three weeks. A neighbor girl, Natalie, practically lived at my house to watch my girls. Sherri was old enough to be terrified and needed me near her, but I could not be there for her. I felt I was experiencing my last moments with Steve.

Yet it was hard to be with Steve. My voice and touch, unlike the nurses who worked with Steve, stimulated his brain, aggravating the swelling. Consequently, I was not allowed to touch or speak to him. In spite of the barbiturate coma, the intentional lack of stimulation, and the passage of time, Steve's brain continued to swell each day.

A monitor attached to his brain beeped out numbers, indicating the degree of swelling. When they surpassed a certain level, it indicated increased swelling—enlargement that was damag-ing Steve's brain. It was agonizing to watch his brain be destroyed piece by piece. Doctors removed a portion of his frontal lobe to make more room for swelling. I was told that Steve had lost all movement on his left side, his ability to communicate, feel emotions, and comprehend words.

My mom arrived shortly after Steve's accident. At first I thought it would be helpful to have her there. She could help me with the girls, drive the car, and answer calls. These were not areas in which she excelled, and it became apparent to both of us in a short time that she was not able to help me in the manner I needed. Consequently, she did not stay long. While she was at my house, she told me a dream about Steve. He was very happy and felt free. He told her that he was concerned about how upset everyone was, and he wanted her to tell us that he had never felt happier, freer. In the dream my mom asked Steve if he was going to come back to us. He replied that it had not yet been decided. She then told him that people were going to have a hard time believing that she had really talked to him. She asked for a way to verify that this information was truly coming from him. He told her to ask the hospital for the clothes he was wearing at the time of his accident. He said they were sitting in a brown plastic bag. With them she would also find his cowboy boots and his wallet.

After she told me about her dream, I found these items being kept by the hospital in a brown plastic bag. It was a sad and hard message to hear, although on a higher level it was comforting. When I held Steve's blood-soaked clothes, I could feel fear emanating from them.

Day after day I waited, not knowing if I were facing Steve's death, long-term rehabilitation, or endless coma. I brought the children to see their dad on two occasions. Sherri told me the only way she was sure it was her dad was that he had dirty fingernails and his little finger was gone. Steve's nails were always dirty from working on engines, and his finger had been amputated in a car accident when he was a teen-ager.

Finally, on September 25, I went to Steve. Totally exhausted, I yelled at him, "If you are going to die, then die. If you are going to live, live. But make a decision. We can't continue any longer. The kids and I are completely drained and exhausted. If you want to die, you have my permission. I love you, but I don't know if I have the energy for another rehabilitation."

Steve's comatose body let out a big sigh. He had heard me. He died three days later, after twenty days in intensive care, with two-thirds of his brain damaged. When he was pronounced dead, I was finally allowed to touch him, hold him, and say good-bye.

[21]

My minister Don Clark had telephoned the house several times since Steve's accident, but I had not returned his calls. I hadn't been to church very often since my injury. Although Don came to give me healings while I was in the hospital, I didn't feel I knew him well. After Steve died, I had to decide how to bury him. He had always liked the idea of a memorial service. One was held for his mother after her death. I was grateful that Don Clark had reached out to me during this time, so I finally called and asked him to preside at the memorial service.

He later told me it was a challenging request because of the diverse audience. Steve's sober biker friends arrived on their Harley Davidson motorcycles, wearing X-Wino patches on their jackets. A few bikers from the drinking days came, too. Several of Steve's relatives and my Aunt Dorothy with her family attended, bringing traditional expectations about funerals. Steve's dad and sister, along with my brother and his family, came with immense grief. Our baby-sitter Natalie and her family and my personal friends were there also. At one point during the service, several bikers stood up and expressed their love for Steve. Their sincerity and Don's gift of prayer reached each diverse heart.

It was very moving, but I was just going through the motions. My brain didn't function, and I felt empty inside, lonely, scared, and confused. I was tired and angry. I was a widow at the age of twenty-nine with two small children. Stephanie was three, insecure, frightened, sad, and confused about her daddy being gone forever. Forever didn't even exist for her. Sherri, six, was shattered. Her daddy had promised to take her roller-skating for her birthday.

"He wouldn't break a promise," she said to all of us. Who was going to protect her, who was going to be her daddy? She wouldn't let anyone get close; it was too risky right now.

People wanted to help. Many showed they cared. I was told that time would heal us, that this was a new beginning. I knew they were right, but I wondered how I would get through one day. How would I live with a hole in me? Whom would I love now? Whom would I hold? For whom would I buy silly things, cook, get dressed? Who would be there for me at night? Who would protect me, know me, love me, argue with me? I hated this. I was not functional, not in control of myself. I was drowning in me, myself, and I. How would I ask for what I needed or even know what I needed? How do I not run away? How could I grieve quickly, keep from blocking my feelings, and still survive the scars? How could I hold my head up high when my neck was so weak? It was quiet, but I could hear myself screaming.

I prayed, "God, You promised me freedom from bondage, peace within, and love. Is this so abstract that I won't be able to touch it? I want something tangible, something solid. Something that tastes good, smells good, feels good, listens, and responds. Is this not in divine order? God, You told me a long time ago that You were going to take Steve away. How could I have understood what that really would mean to me and my children? Couldn't You have found another way? I feel so empty, abandoned, forsaken. Remember that I am a woman. I am here. Lonely, vulnerable, naked. God, hold me tight. I feel lost. Where are You? Why are You so quiet?"

After the memorial service, I asked Dawn if she would move in with me for a while. She seemed so calm. I felt she would be a grounding influence in the home. It would also be nice to have some company.

Dawn agreed but would not be able to come immediately. During that interval I found it difficult to eat although everybody brought food with them when they visited. Sleep came as hard as eating. I lay on the couch instead of the bed. It was more tolerable in the living room.

My brother took my girls with him for a few days. When I was left alone, I made a decision to drink. I was on my way out to buy a bottle when Pat arrived with two friends. They had come to mow the grass. I waited inside for them to finish. They seemed to take forever. Finally I heard the lawn mower stop. They came to the door and asked if they could have a cup of coffee. I was so angry with them. I thought, "Why won't they leave?"

Pat said to me, "You know, while we were mowing the grass, it occurred to us that you are recovering, too. We wondered if you were thinking about drinking?"

They stayed for a while and talked to me about how important it would be for me to talk about my pain and reach out to people. Before they left, they all made themselves available if I needed to talk. It wrecked my plan to buy a bottle. I called Pat later that day and asked him to come back over. I was ready to start sharing.

I quit school with only two weeks left of my first

internship. It didn't matter any more. I couldn't concentrate. I also quit using my Bassett electromagnetic stimulator. Nothing mattered.

Sherri was starting first grade. She needed school supplies. The insanity of school supplies being important when I was dying inside made me cry. I called Pat and told him I hadn't eaten in three days. My leg hurt too much to walk on it, and I had to get Sherri school supplies. He told me he would send help.

A little while later Steve's friend Doc walked in. He seemed like a giant of a man, with disheveled hair, a scraggly beard, and a heart of gold. I knew Doc, but I had never been alone with him. I found him a little scary until he sat down and said "No problem" in response to my situation. He picked me up and carried me to his car. He took me out to eat and shoved food in my mouth, one bite at a time. Then he took me to Target, a local discount store. He put me in a shopping cart and pushed me around while we got the school supplies. He made me laugh and saved the day.

Pat joined us on Sherri's birthday so we could take her roller-skating. It was a hard day, and I was glad he was there. Sherri was mad that Pat came along and sad that her dad wasn't there. We all just went through the motions, our hearts broken. This celebration crystallized the reality of Steve's absence.

On September 30, the day that Steve would have been thirty-one, I left for a short trip to Virginia Beach. Once I was on the plane, I felt peaceful. I was finally able to relax. When I arrived, I went directly to the beach and lay on the sand. I stayed for several hours listening to the roar of the ocean, feeling it pull on my feet. I touched the sand over and over again as I watched the sea gulls fly in and out of the waves catching their dinner. I slept. I felt sad. I felt awe at the massiveness of the world and all its possibilities.

Carolyn and I talked, and I realized how angry I was at Steve for leaving me. At the Health Services Department, my massage therapist told me she was concerned about my leg. There was green stuff coming out of a small sore. She tried unsuccessfully to set up an appointment for me with a doctor she respected. It didn't work out, and it didn't matter to me.

On my second night, I met Ron on the steps going into the A.R.E. library. His gentleness attracted me. We talked briefly, and I asked him if he would like to have dinner with me. He thanked me, but he already had a date. The next day we saw each other again, and we went for a walk on the beach. We talked, and he held me. It felt so good to be held. I believed that God had sent me a comforter. That night I went out with Carolyn. After I got home, Ron knocked on my door. He stayed for a while and made love to me. He was a gentle and sensitive lover. I became engulfed in the moment and briefly I felt alive again. Thank You, Father.

[22]

I decided to sell the house. Steve and I had bought it from a wonderful real estate man who liked to help young couples purchase their starter home. I felt he was a trustworthy man with good values, so I asked him to sell my house to some young couple just starting out, like Steve and I had been. The first open house was set for October 10.

Stephanie had a massive asthma attack that kept us both up for three night before the open house. It affirmed for me that it was a good idea to leave. On the morning of the tenth, I awoke to find that to put my leg down off the bed caused tremendous pain. It was so intense that I could not tolerate it for a moment and had to elevate my leg immediately. I called Dr. Gustillo, and he asked me to come into the hospital. I told him I didn't want to go to the hospital again, and he said that was the only place I could get his help. There was no choice. I couldn't stay on the bed forever. Dawn volunteered to watch the girls, and I went to emergency assisted by a friend.

Going back to the hospital was hard. As I lay in my bed waiting to meet my new doctors, all I could think about was that Steve had died in this hospital and I didn't want to be here.

As it turned out, Doctor Lindqueist—my most favorite doctor in the world—was in charge of my case. Thank You, God. He told me there was a staph infection in my leg. When I was released the previous May, I had been told to come back in a month and not to bear weight on my leg. The little brace they had given me had been only a temporary protection while I was out on reprieve. An immediate amputation might have been the result of my stubbornness in not coming back and the constant weight bearing down on my grossly unstable leg.

I was left alone for the first two days, probably because it was a weekend. No medical orders had been written about me yet. Whatever the reason, it gave me a chance to rest and grieve. I rested and cried; then I cried and rested. By Monday I had decided amputation was the only way out of this mess. Doctor Lindqueist and Doctor Gustillo confirmed my decision, telling me they had used virtually every orthopedic procedure they knew to try to heal my leg. Everything had been unsuccessful. They had only one more idea to try, and if it didn't work, they recommended amputation. They wanted to insert a rod inside my tibia. This would hold the tibia rigid so it could heal, and it would bring live bone cells down to the site of non-union. Conditions were complicated by large calluses that had formed at the ends of each piece of my tibia, right at the point where there needed to be a union. This procedure would open the calluses, allowing a better environment for the union to occur.

When Doctor Lindqueist and I were alone, I asked him not to do any more procedures on me. I told him I needed to go home and be a mom to my kids. I was all they had now, and I couldn't be coming back into the hospital over and over again. Doctor Lindqueist promised me that when he did the procedure, he would follow through only if everything seemed to be going well. He wouldn't use any heroics and he wouldn't force something that didn't want to happen. If it appeared to him that this was a waste of time in any way, he would go ahead and amputate. I trusted Doctor Lindqueist to follow divine guidance.

I spent the next couple of days preparing for amputation. A lady came to teach me about prosthetics, and amputation became more of a reality for me. David, who had now become my lawyer representing Steve's wrongful death action, stopped by with a will for me to sign before I had surgery. He said if I died during surgery without a will, it would create a difficult situation. The floor nurses witnessed my signature.

I didn't read it; I didn't care. David told me briefly what it entailed, and it mainly had to do with money. I told him whom I wanted to have custody of my daughters, and he assured me that that was indicated in the will. Nothing else mattered at that point to me.

I had a talk with Doctor Lindqueist about divine justice. I told him that I thought I should be able to die during surgery. It seemed like the "just" thing to happen. He didn't agree with my interpretation of the Lord's justice.

Much to my surprise, I awoke from surgery with my toes still attached. Doctor Lindqueist told me that everything had gone very smoothly. Now, all I had to do was to survive a stretch of I.V. antibiotics and I could go home.

I had many visitors, Pat and Doc among them. I sold my house during this hospitalization and kept in touch with Dawn and the kids on a daily basis.

On October 18, while still hospitalized, I had a dream acknowledging my inner child for the first time. In this dream I carried Stephanie to her crib and Sherri to her bed. Then I remembered a third child. I was shocked to realize I had a third. I went outside, and when I found her, she looked neglected, with dirty torn clothing and disheveled hair. Her eyes were deep and full of a sadness that comes from abandonment. However, I had the sense that she didn't know that she had been abandoned. It was as though she knew life only as she had lived it, expecting no more.

I felt guilty for ignoring her all these years, and I took her home. She was younger than Stephanie and needed a crib to sleep in. I thought of how I had created safe places for Sherri and Stephanie to lay their heads at night, and this child had not even been given a corner in my house. I wondered how I would tell Sherri and Stephanie about her. I also wondered how she had survived. She needed so much nurturing, it overwhelmed me to think of this added responsibility. A piece of me knew that I couldn't deny her any more. In the dream I had a distant memory that she was my child. But even though I knew I was her mother, still we were strangers.

This dream was a very small beginning to a very long inner healing process. At this moment in my life, the child felt safe enough to appear to me. With Steve gone and I myself having decided to live, I could now be attentive to her needs. In spite of this initial appearance, it was years before I was able to be aware of my little girl on a daily basis. Yet it was through her that I found the creativity to write this story.

Under the protection of Doctor Lindqueist, with prayers and support from many friends, I made it through the I.V. antibiotic treatment. I continued to be aware that only a little over a month earlier my husband had died in this very hospital, and it was not a place I wanted to be.

On October 27, my friend Donna collected me from the hospital. I wore a full-length cast that went from my upper thigh to the bottom of my foot. As we went up the driveway to my house, a very present reality hit me: Steve wouldn't be there to greet me. I remembered the last time I returned from the hospital. I was greeted by a sign—made from one of my sheets—on the outside of the house. There was no sign today; no joyful reception. The house was empty, surrounded by a cloud of grief. We both felt it.

Dawn had left, and the children were away: Sherri was at school, Stephanie with friends. Donna stayed until they came home. Both friends whom I had asked to come and spend the night with me called and cancelled. I was exhausted and in pain, both physically and emotionally. How are we going to do this? I wondered.

On that first night home, Sherri got a stomach flu. She woke me up to say that she had vomited in her bed. I was incapable of helping her, and I suggested she sleep in the living room. A little while later she woke me again to say she had vomited in the living room. The only place left for her to sleep was on the floor, and that is where she finished the night.

I felt totally beaten. My prayer to God that night was, "If You think You can run this place, do it. Clean up the vomit. Go ahead, I can't. I surrender. I have no more solutions or answers. My life is totally in Your hands."

The next morning I received a phone call from my public health nurse informing me that I was eligible for house-cleaning services. She wondered if I might need them.

[23]

The next few months were lived an hour at a time. I found a townhouse to buy, and we moved after Christmas. Pat was very supportive and made himself available to me. Grandpa, the leader of the X-Winos, also became a good friend and was a source of strength on which I relied. Many of Steve's biker friends would stop by just to say hello and to see if I needed anything. My girlfriends kept in touch and made sure that I got out of the house once in a while. I started to go to dances and think in terms of dating.

When Steve died, I was blessed with large sums of money that came from a variety of insurance policies we had taken out, including a private life insurance policy and a policy through his union. A mortgage insurance policy paid off the house. All this money freed me from thinking about having to find paid employment for a while.

On December 17 I went to the clinic to check the progress of my leg. It had been two months since my surgery, and I had been told I would be wearing my cast for about six months. After X-rays were taken, Doctor Gustillo and Doctor Lindqueist came into my room and surprisingly announced that my tibia had united and I didn't need to return. The cast was taken off, and I said my good-byes to the hospital. It was my thirtieth birthday.

Although the doctors had accomplished a lot, my leg still needed help. The coloring was unhealthy: a sickly, greyish white. There was so much swelling that at times I couldn't put on a shoe, and I still experienced pain when I walked. I wondered what would become of my leg if it didn't improve.

The New Year came in painfully. I attended a gathering at my church. In the middle of it, I had to leave because I couldn't stop the tears. The minister's wife stopped me on my way out and said, "Don't be ashamed of your tears. They represent how deeply you loved Steve."

I heard about a couple named George and Mary-Jo who had started a recovery program in the mission called "Christ Center." At first curiosity led me to find them and see what they were doing at the mission. Once I experienced Mary-Jo, I knew she could help me survive this time in my life. I asked her if I could come and do volunteer work at Christ Center. It was a program for street alcoholics who had unsuccessfully tried other recovery programs. George and Mary-Jo wanted to work only with those folks who knew there was no other place they could go. I felt as if I fit that description. Even though I was successfully staying sober, my sobriety felt shaky. Mary-Jo explained to me that they offered two resources for recovery: the twelve steps of Alcoholics Anonymous and Jesus Christ. It didn't matter to them which vehicle was chosen because, in their eyes, both led to the same place.

I had always had trouble acknowledging Jesus. Mary-Jo put Him in terms that I could accept. "Jesus is a wonderful man who offers friendship to those who want it." That didn't seem so scary to me. With that in mind, I could comfortably sing the gospel songs and listen to the praises that were constantly being given to Jesus. Before, I had always felt uncomfortable and pressured when people talked about their love for Jesus.

Mary-Jo told me I was everything she didn't need. A young, pretty widow who was vulnerable and needy. She continued, "The Lord works in mysterious ways because I also know that you were sent to me by Him. You can come and work for me if the brothers agree."

The brothers were the folks who were participating in the recovery program. The mission was not accustomed to women being around, and I was told never to walk through the mission alone. A brother was always to accompany me. On my first day, Mary-Jo told me the best way to get to know the brothers was to spend some time with them. She left me in a room full of men sitting on overstuffed chairs and sofas, and she told me to circulate. I looked around at the men in the room and felt self-conscious and out of place. The only idea that occurred to me was to play a game of cards. I asked if they would like to play cards, and that was my beginning back to life.

I went to the mission about four or five hours a day, four days a week. The brothers called me Sister Gayle, and they taught me how to survive. These folks had survived conditions beyond my imagination, and they still knew how to laugh and love. After a short time, they looked forward to my arrival in the morning, and I looked forward to going. I soon discovered ways to make their lives brighter.

One brother liked me to drive him to a fried chicken take-out restaurant for his favorite food. Another took pride in teaching me his favorite card game and whipping me every time we played. Some of them shared personal stories that were full of hope and gratitude. When a new man joined the program, the seasoned brothers took him aside and explained how he was to treat me, like a sister. I felt very protected.

One of the younger brothers, who was about twenty-four, suggested that we make some nutritional food and have a pot luck dinner. He introduced me to ghee—clarified butter—and later asked me if I would consider dating him. It was the first professional boundary issue I had to confront. I was also flattered that he would find me appealing in my dilapidated state. Mary-Jo helped me to find the right words to communicate: "No, but thank you." My heart responded to these men, and I could feel that it was beginning to heal. Along with that healing, my hope and faith were being renewed.

In February, I went back to Virginia Beach to visit Carolyn. While I was there, I decided that this would be a great place for the girls and me to heal our hearts. The A.R.E. had started an experimental grade school that would offer the understanding my children needed, along with some unique learning experiences. I thought I could try Cayce remedies in order to improve the condition of my leg. Cayce recommended many holistic treatments in his readings, including castor oil packs, osteopathic adjustments, massage oil mixtures, prayer, dietary changes, exercise, and affirmations. They had effectively helped many people with a variety of health problems. I even remembered the "castor oil beds" that Jo had described to me many months ago.

I felt it might be time now to apply the Cayce health information. But I knew I needed support and guidance if I was to be successful. The A.R.E. headquarters seemed to be the perfect place to find that support and all the information I would require. I also thought it would be nice to take a break from the constant reminders of Steve's death and of my previous leg operations that bombarded us at home. To move the family to Virginia Beach felt like hope for a new beginning. With only three days available to me on this visit, nevertheless, I found and rented a house one block from the beach and the A.R.E. headquarters. It was available for us to move in on July 1.

When I returned to Minnesota, I told the kids that in four months we were moving to the beach for one year. They weren't thrilled, but I knew they would like it once we got there. I decided it would be good to have my school certificate completed before I left. The college reinstated me and allowed me to complete my second internship at the mission under the supervision of Mary-Jo, who was a certified chemical dependency counselor. After completing my second internship, I agreed to return to St. Mary's for one month in order to finish my first internship with Mary Ellen.

That February I also began a certificate program in Chemical Dependency and Family Intimacy through the University of Minnesota Sexuality Department. Months before, during my first internship, I had become aware that it was difficult, if not impossible, for me to discuss sexual concerns with clients. Participating in this program was my way of sorting out my own issues and learning techniques to deal with intimacy matters with clients. Confronting my own issues became overwhelming as this program brought to the surface my own problems with sexuality. I decided to process these new insights with a psychotherapist.

These university classes met for three days, once every two months. I decided to continue the program after moving to Virginia but that required flying or driving back every two months. Those trips also turned out to be a nice way to stay connected to my friends in Minnesota.

Meanwhile, my lawyer David was developing a lawsuit over Steve's accident. He told me that Steve had been driving home on the freeway when he came upon a sign that stated "Construction next thirteen miles." There was no machinery around or construction warning devices such as lights, barricades, or cones. It was after sunset, and Steve approached an accident shortly after passing this sign. David felt safe in assuming, from testimony by two other bikers who were with Steve, that he could see that the lanes were separated by a ridge. It was the temporary result of one lane having been tarred and the other not. As Steve and his two companions approached the earlier accident, lights from the emergency vehicles lit up the highway. They were waved on past the accident and started down the road again. One-half mile before the end of this construction zone, Steve attempted to pass a car. He hit the ridge and flipped off his bike, landing on his head. When the other bikers got to him, he was unconscious. About the time an ambulance eventually got to him, he regained consciousness and became combative, saying, "Leave me alone. I just want to go home." (I was told later that people often became combative after sustaining head injuries.) Steve was taken to the nearest hospital, where a doctor called me, asking my permission to fly him home.

In his investigation, David learned that there had been five major accidents and perhaps hundreds of minor ones that night along this thirteen-mile stretch of highway. The bike rally at Sturgis, South Dakota, had just ended, and many bikers were heading home. After sunset it was difficult to see the ridge in the road, and bikes started falling left and right as they hit it. Even the previous accident which Steve had bypassed involved the death of a women who had been riding with her husband.

David told me this was a solid case—a lawyer's dream. He was asking $16,000,000 in recovery. I questioned him how he could ask for so much, and he responded, "I can ask for as much as I want, as long as I can justify it." Then he went on to justify it in terms of lost income and emotional distress. He also told me that other lawyers would love to have this case, and he wanted to know if I was willing to stay loyal to him to the end. If I couldn't make that commitment, he didn't want the case. It would involve considerable work, and he wanted to be assured it would be worth it. I couldn't imagine why I would ever want a different lawyer. In my mind David was Steve's lawyer and friend. He had a personal interest in doing the best job he could. I told him I was willing to stay loyal to him to the end.

I didn't hear too much about the case unless David needed me to sign something or find something for him. My interest in the lawsuit was minimal; I was busy with school and trying to move.

I graduated from St. Mary's program in early June. The brothers came to my graduation ceremony and presented me with a gift of clothes that they personally picked out. It was an amazing feat, knowing that they all had no income. I learned early in my work at Christ Center that there were certain things better not to know. So I never asked them how they obtained the present.

Another gift from the brothers was my ability to quit smoking. When they heard I had an acupuncture appointment to quit smoking, a couple of them asked if they could go with me. They said they would like to ask Jesus to take my smoking away. I replied that it was O.K. with me. They could ask Jesus to help me, and I would go for acupuncture. I'll never know for sure exactly what worked, but for the first time after several attempts I walked away from cigarettes.

When it came time for the move to Virginia, my friends from AA gave me a good-bye party. So did my friends from the A.R.E. study group. I rented out my townhouse for a year and packed a small car-top carrier with everything we could possibly bring with us to Virginia Beach. The rest of our belongings went into storage.

I attended the annual X-Wino Turkey Roast the night before we left. All of Steve's biker friends were there, as well as my friend Donna with her family. That night

Donna and Grandpa presented me with my four-year medallion honoring my continuous sobriety. It was a warm feeling to be with those folks again, but it felt like an ending. This was Steve's life, not mine. I felt secure that I would maintain the close friends from this group, even while I was living in Virginia. But that night I was also feeling numb, simply because I had been in constant motion the past few months, preparing for our move. I felt as if I were saying good-bye and doing the right things, but my insides were shut down.

[24]

Our time in Virginia Beach was extremely healing on several levels. I was able to focus in on my leg—using natural remedies—to redefine myself as a single woman, to re-establish a relationship with my children that had been disrupted by trauma, and to heal a measure of the grief that my girls and I carried to Virginia.

Unfortunately, insecurities and self-doubt plagued me mercilessly those first few weeks. The trip to Virginia was nerve racking. The reality of what I had done hit me while I lay in the motel bed on the first night. I had left all my friends. How would my needs be met in a strange place? A part of me wanted to turn around and forget the whole thing. The other part of me knew I would be in pain anywhere I went, and I recognized that Virginia Beach was a place my children and I would have a chance to heal. The ocean, the sun, and the A.R.E. would be at our fingertips. They were resources that I didn't have in Minnesota.

When I had visited the beach in February, I talked

about houses with my friend Carolyn. I told her that I thought a red-brick kitchen floor seemed welcoming to me. She said that she knew of a house for rent on 70th Street, and it would be available in July. The current occupants were healers. I felt very clearly that this was the perfect house for me and my girls. At that moment July seemed like a great time for us to come; the house was one block from the ocean and two blocks from the A.R.E. When I walked into the house for the first time, I immediately noticed that the kitchen had a red-brick linoleum floor.

But now several months had gone by since I had signed the lease. Now we were actually moving. The clarity was gone when I walked into the house on July 1. I was exhausted from three days of driving with the girls and all their questions. We unloaded the car, changed into our bathing suits, and went right to the beach. The salt air, the sound of the surf, and the feel of the sand in my toes reminded me of why I had made this decision. Sherri and Stephanie were delighted that they had this wonderful beach practically in their backyard.

Although the house had a welcoming, warm energy to it, I still found a need to sleep in the living room. Bedrooms felt too isolated for my aching heart. I purchased a rollaway and put it in the living room to be used as a couch and a bed for me.

Within a short time, I began to feel the loss of the support system that I had left in Minnesota. I took in boarders to help fill the void. My first boarder was Lynn. She had returned to Virginia Beach to work in the A.R.E. summer day-camp program. She was an Italian from Maryland who had a great deal of energy, and the girls loved her. She roomed with Stephanie and stayed all summer with us.

The girls participated in the day camp. It helped them meet people and get comfortable with the ocean and their new surroundings. Stephanie fell in love with sand crabs. Her first day at the beach she brought one home in her towel, pleading a case about them being great pets. The next day she brought back another one and told me that Sam, her first sand crab, must have had a baby. Her camp counselor informed me that she filled her towel with them one day, but they weren't discovered in time to save them from dehydration.

A neighbor gave me two kittens, and the girls were delighted. Sherri's was a fluffy orange kitten that she named Cocoa; Stephanie's was a short-haired Tortie that was black, brown, and orange. She named this second kitten Crusty because he reminded her of toast. I liked having a house full of people and pets. It helped with the loneliness, and Lynn was great with the kids. It freed me up to go to AA meetings and to date once in a while.

Before our move, whenever I thought of coming to Virginia Beach, I pictured it to be a place where I would find happiness. On previous visits, I had experienced a strong healing energy there, and those trips usually left me feeling happy. My anticipatory image appeared to be reasonable to me. However, there was one item I hadn't considered about happiness: it had to come from within me, and I didn't know who "me" was. Since the age of fourteen, I had found my identity through Steve. Here no one knew Steve; virtually no one knew about my accident or that I was a widow. I was on my own with no history and no support system to protect me. When I entered a room, nobody said, "Hi, Gayle." All that history and support that I found so suffocating back home would have been welcomed during those first few months.

I began the process of defining myself by exploring my sexuality. Actually, the seeds of this process were planted during the last few months of my marriage. Steve and I reached levels of intimacy that I had not experienced before. After he died, while I was still in

Minnesota, I began attracting sexual partners, and this continued soon after I arrived in Virginia Beach. Unfortunately, I attracted men who weren't emotionally healthy and found myself in some abusive situations. It forced me to start setting some boundaries and to define my values. The immediate result of this process was that I became more selective in choosing sexual partners. Eventually I chose abstinence in order to allow myself some time to heal and to grow.

AA played a significant role in my healing process while I was in Virginia. It provided me with immediate access to people, and it forced me to stay focused on my recovery from alcoholism. Leaving my group in Minnesota had been a difficult adjustment. I had been with that group for four years. They had seen me through my accident and Steve's death. In Virginia I was a new face, and they had a different style of meetings. On one of my previous trips to Virginia Beach, I had attended an AA meeting, thought it was great, and was surprised at all its similarities to the one back home. But now that I was living here, I was much more critical and I focused in on the differences. I learned quickly that a criticizing newcomer from another state is not well received. People told me, "It's the same twelve steps of recovery, and it's up to you what you do with them." I eventually came around to believe it myself, and I found many friends once I stopped trying to remake Virginia AA.

This turnabout was triggered by one especially tough day. On August 28, the first anniversary of Steve's death, my resistance to AA still kept me from forming a strong support system. I found myself in the depths of grief again. My body was screaming for a drink. I envisioned myself running as fast as I could to escape the pain.

In the resort-hotel section of Virginia Beach, businesses rented mopeds to tourists to ride around town. I rented one and went at top speed (which was about forty miles per hour) for a two-hour bike ride. The engine sounded whiny compared to the roar of a Harley, and the speed was considerably slower, but my position of driver—instead of the familiar one as passenger on a bike—was significantly helpful. I felt in control and empowered by being the driver. As I buzzed down the country roads, I let the tears fall. I prayed that a car would come out of nowhere and strike me dead. My defiance soared as I read the sticker attached to the bike: "Only to be driven within one mile of town." I wasn't sure where I was, but I had passed the one-mile limit twenty minutes ago. That bike ride kept me sober one more day, and that night I went to an AA meeting and shared my grief. It was the first night I let my barriers down enough to feel the group's support.

In that AA meeting, I remembered one of the brothers at the Union Gospel Mission. Ralph had touched my heart. I had mentioned to him that I was feeling like drinking. He told me, "You know, the trouble with going back out there and getting loaded is that sooner or later you have to get sober again. I know, I've tried to stay drunk forever. To realize what has happened and how far down you've gone—it's a thought that helps me stay away from that first drink." Ralph's words helped me that August night in Virginia, too.

I wasn't the only one in the family having some rough times. Before we left Minnesota, Stephanie's asthma had gotten steadily worse. She was being treated at Children's Hospital in St. Paul on a regular basis, requiring hospital stays that kept getting longer and occurring more frequently. The last time she was hospitalized, she was there five days before making any significant improvement. I went to visit her one day during this stay, and she told me she was going to go where her dad had gone. I started to cry. I told her she couldn't go because if she went, I would die, and then Sherri would be left alone. I needed her to stay with me. I pleaded with her to stay with me.

As we prepared to leave for Virginia, the doctors put

her on prednisone (a form of cortisone) to help her make the trip without an attack. Once we arrived, I was immediately to find a doctor who could help her be weaned from the prednisone and treat her with other drugs. Once we arrived, I thought of how foolish I had been to bring her to a strange town. How would I ever find a doctor who would understand the trauma we had experienced and treat Stephanie and me with a gentle manner?

Again the Lord sent me exactly what I needed. A neighbor lady told me about a wonderful pediatrician who was called affectionately "Dr. Sue." She managed to keep Stephanie out of the hospital throughout our year in Virginia. It was a miracle considering what we had been through in Minnesota. Stephanie still struggled with her asthma, but we were able to treat her with medications and home care.

That summer I spent more time with my children than I had in a long time. Few people distracted me, and no hospital visits took me away. I have always been a task-oriented person, so I filled our summer days with fun adventures on the beach and around the community. We made drip sand castles and sand sculptures. We took long walks on the beach looking for exciting treasures. We feasted on crab and lobster. We drove to Colonial Williamsburg and across the Chesapeake Bay Bridge. We learned about tides, sand crabs, sunburn, and "nor'easters"—damaging coastal storms. Our summer was full of novel experiences that filled our heads with new thoughts.

Even though I found this time with my children healing, it was challenging to be around them so much. One of the unresolved issues that presented itself again this summer was a longstanding struggle I had with Sherri. Previously Steve had seen it and confronted me on it. In some ways Sherri and I were similar: we both were verbal people and took life seriously; and we both had strong emotional reactions. But these similarities didn't rid me of my irritations. I would pick on the qualities in her that were different from mine. For example, Sherri tended to be more concerned with details than I, and she took time to value things that I hardly even acknowledged. She also had an innate ability to perceive the subtle quality of things: she noticed colors, textures, and smells. In many ways this was a wonderful trait, but it could also be irritating when she found the color, smell, or texture unpleasant. It especially became a point of tension for us in situations where I didn't even consciously notice these things. Sometimes I wondered if I really loved her. It left me feeling guilty and angry that love didn't come as easily as with Stephanie. Slowly I came to an important realization: my reactions to Sherri had a lot to do with my struggle trying to like myself. Sherri no longer irritated me when my own self-love emerged.

On August 22 I had a dream that helped me turn this relationship around. In the dream I was driving with Sherri in a sports car along a flooded road. I drove back and forth three times. The third time I said, "That's enough," at which point my tires slipped on the watery pavement, and the car slid into the ocean. It was dark under the water. I could see only black. As my body was pulled down deeper, I heard myself clearly say to Sherri, "Swim upwards until you reach the top." When I got to the top, Sherri was not there. I got aboard a boat and saw a phone. I called my friend Fran and frantically pleaded, "Fran, help me. Sherri has drowned."

I awoke from this dream sobbing. I could feel the grief as if the dream had been real. There was no longer any doubt in my mind about how much I loved Sherri. I went to her room and woke her up. Through my tears I said to her, "Sherri, if you ever fall in the ocean, swim up. Do you hear me? Swim up."

She was so sleepy and confused she merely mumbled, "Yes, Mommy, I will." The memory of that dream never left me. The following days reflected my new tolerance toward our differences.

Differences among family members were not the only ones that I faced. I noticed cultural distinctions between Minnesotans and Virginians. The southern influence in Virginia was foreign to me. The dynamics between men and women were different. It seemed to me that the women tended to charm the men and encourage them to feel virile, while the men liked to be in charge and to think of women as the weaker sex. When I was in social situations, I felt like a bull in a china closet because I didn't have the social graces that seemed to be spoon-fed from birth to these southern women. Of course, hanging out with bikers had probably roughened up my edges a bit.

The friendliness at every turn reminded me of what I envisioned as "southern hospitality." In Minnesota people weren't quick to be friendly. So when a Virginian expressed this "southern hospitality," I didn't feel comfortable or know how to respond. The directness that I experienced back home was not to be found in Virginia. Here, people spoke with a tactful charm that confused me. I also encountered a negative attitude toward "Yankees," a term not even in my vocabulary before coming to Virginia.

These cultural differences were most noticeable at first, when I already felt like an outsider. As time went by and I felt more secure, my hypercritical nature calmed down. I began to adapt to the different style of communication, although I never felt that I attained the level of femininity that I perceived in these Virginia women.

Shortly after we arrived, I set up an appointment with Nancy, a nurse who was in charge of the A.R.E. Health Services Department. Here I had received massages and colonics on previous visits. I assumed the A.R.E. would be as excited as I was to work on healing my leg. Nancy told me they didn't treat patients in this department; they only offered an opportunity for people to experience some of the Cayce remedies. Two doctors in Arizona had set up a medical clinic to treat people for specific ailments. But Nancy indicated that if I wanted to work with her, she would do so during her off hours.

We set up a program and format to document our progress. I mentioned to Nancy the use of "castor oil beds," described by Jo several months ago. She was aware of Jo's work and agreed that putting my leg in a castor oil pack all night would be advantageous. I was to wear such a pack on my leg all night long for four consecutive nights—then I would take three nights off. This was a weekly cycle I kept up.

Because we decided to follow Cayce's holistic format—working with body, mind, and spirit—Nancy and I looked for mental/spiritual approaches, too. We created an affirmation based on the one from my dream when I was in the hospital:

> Thank you, leg, for staying, for growing back together. It took a lot of courage on the cells' part. I would like to ask you to recall the memory of how you looked in your original healthy and whole state and try to manifest that state again. Thank You, God, for the perfection of my left leg, its circulation, its muscle and nerve structure, and its perfectly beautiful skin.

We put the affirmation on several cards, then pasted on each card a magazine picture of healthy legs. These cards were placed throughout my house to help me remember to say the affirmation and to visualize my leg as healed.

I received weekly massages to stimulate circulation and enhance total body functioning. We consistently evaluated my diet, trying to maintain an alkaline environment in my system. I also started taking supplemental vitamins and minerals. To strengthen my leg I initiated an exercise program, consisting mainly of walking and biking because that was all I was motivated to do. I also agreed to follow a regular schedule for daily meditation and prayer.

Nancy had a friend who periodically took photos of my leg. At regular intervals Nancy took measurements of my ankle, calf, knee, and thigh. At first my knee and ankle were almost always swollen. Our goal was to decrease those measurements. An increase for my thigh and calf were also targets, dependent on success with muscle development. Nancy not only donated her off-duty time to help me establish and monitor this program of healing, she also supported me emotionally during the process. She was enthusiastic about our goals and consistently found ways to affirm progress. Her high energy and positive attitudes made a big impression—and I learned that she had made some hard decisions in her life to gain more inner peace. She was committed to healing, and often I gained my strength through her faith in our project.

My support system was starting to emerge, and many of my goals were being addressed. With summer coming to a close, I was curious how it would feel to be at Virginia Beach when the tourists and conferees went home.

[25]

We started settling in by September. When the girls began at Greenwood—A.R.E.'s experimental grade school—it put more structure into our days. Stephanie participated in their preschool program, and Sherri was in second grade. Lynn moved out with the arrival of fall, and I took a break from boarders. I found the days too long and started doing volunteer work for a city-run, daytime program for alcoholics.

I was beginning to reap some of the benefits from my work with Nancy. The castor oil packs had decreased the swelling in my knee and ankle, which in turn diminished my pain and increased my mobility. We continued to pursue our original program, making minor adjustments in my diet and exercises as needed. The color of my leg was also starting to improve. It lost the greyish tinge. My normal skin became tan; and the scar tissue, pink. But this was going to be no quick and easy process. For example, the scar tissue was so severe that we felt we should continue my recovery program for at least a year.

The improvement in my leg freed me to walk longer distances on a regular basis. Sherri, Stephanie, and I started taking hikes in the cypress gardens. We would pack a snack and make up fun games as our spirits were filled by the magical energy that seemed to permeate the trails. The weather stayed mild throughout the year, and I found myself much more active than I had ever been in Minnesota. Often we would go for walks on the beach as the kids shared their experiences from their days at school.

One of my favorite school stories concerned an injured duck in a nearby pond. The children were told to pray for the duck and have their families pray, too. Sherri gave me instructions about my role in this experiment, and daily I received reports on the healing progress. What a lucky duck! It healed quite well with all those prayers. This was but one of many experiences for the children at Greenwood School about the power of prayer and visualization.

The classes Sherri and Stephanie attended were small and intimate. Their teachers were sensitive to the nature of children. Sherri was angry about her dad dying and would often act it out. I saw the teachers stretch themselves to respect Sherri's suffering and still maintain boundaries for the pain. I believe the intimate, caring environment allowed Sherri to feel safe enough to act out her feelings. In a traditional school system, she would have been shamed and disciplined. Her pain would never have been addressed.

My girls thought this was a very strange school because it did not have a lunch room or a gymnasium. They brought their lunches and the beach was their gym. But their smiling faces and the fullness of their experiences at school told me that they were healing.

That fall the girls and I experienced our first "nor'easter," the local term for coastal storms having strong northeast winds and huge beach-eroding waves. Some places reported twenty-foot crests. The rain eventually flooded many streets. Signs were blown away, and the roof rattled all night. We went down near the oceanfront during the storm, and green foam flew on us like snow. The tidal surges came right up to the houses, and we thought it was very exciting. The whole thing reminded me of Minnesota tornados, but this storm lasted three days. Amazingly the local people acted as if it were no big deal.

On Sherri's birthday, I decided to make her cake from scratch. It was one of those days when everything went wrong. Someone might have thought it was my first cake. With my clothing spattered with cake batter, I made a mad dash to the store to purchase an easy box cake and icing. There I met Dan, whom I had not seen since my move to Virginia. I was embarrassed by how I looked, but he was as charming as ever. Once I forgot about my appearance, I noticed that my previous strong attraction for him had completely disappeared. We chatted for a while, parted cordially, and I left knowing this chapter in my life was definitely closed.

I started going to singles' functions put together by Julie, my massage therapist and friend. Julie and I met in AA, but she was also interested in the work that went on at the A.R.E. When she first started giving me massages, she told me she thought my leg was a miracle, and she was excited to be a part of its healing. She may not have realized what an important part she was playing in helping me heal another aspect of my life: human relations. It seemed that most of my friends and acquaintances in Virginia Beach were in relationships, so I was glad that Julie organized some singles' activities. They were specifically for people who were committed to sobriety. The first event was a potluck at her house followed by an ocean swim. A new guy named Kurt appeared. It was his first day sober. He looked like a young surfer, and it was hard to tell that he had suffered from alcoholism because he was in great physical shape. He was over six feet tall and had an Irish look to him: sparkling eyes, freckles, and a charming smile. I purposely didn't pay much attention to him because he was attractive and brand new to sobriety, a dangerous combination if I ever saw one.

He started appearing at the various AA meetings I attended. One Friday we all went dancing after the meeting. Kurt was in the group. I offered to drive a few folks home, and Kurt was the last to get dropped off. He opened the door to get out, then turned and looked at me. I asked him if there was something he wanted, and he leaned over and kissed me. The kiss was no peck on the cheek, and it took me totally by surprise. Not that I hadn't been attracted to Kurt. I had, but I had made a conscious effort not to connect with him. He asked me to come into his apartment for a while. I did, and we continued to kiss. It was great, until I remembered the commitment to myself about being selective and establishing good boundaries. I decided to go home. He couldn't believe it. This made no sense to him at all.

I went home and decided once again that new sobriety and good looks were out of bounds for me. A person new to sobriety is in transition and rarely has the stability for romantic relationships. It was my thirty-first birthday.

[26]

As 1982 came to a close, I decided to change work sites. The city program in which I was a volunteer was run by social workers. In my opinion, they didn't understand alcoholism. They believed that by giving an alcoholic a job and some clothes they would motivate that person to stay sober. The basis of their thinking was that alcoholism was a motivational problem, not a disease.

I had heard about a halfway house in Portsmouth, about thirty minutes' drive away, run by a recovering man named Hal. When we met, Hal invited me on board, and I accepted. I started as a volunteer, but Hal soon hired me as an assistant counselor. After about two months, my immediate supervisor told me that Hal was interested in me as a woman, not as an employee. Hal was married and clearly out of bounds for me. I was frustrated that he wouldn't let my work be the focus of our interactions. I sought out a new position immediately. Within a month I was working as an assistant counselor in an inpatient alcoholism program at a psychiatric hospital in Portsmouth. This was a quality program, and I enjoyed my work there.

Meanwhile, we took on another boarder named Virginia. She was from England and came to Virginia Beach for a few months to work on projects for her church. She was bright, imaginative, and very helpful. It was through her that we had the opportunity to meet her friends who had also come: Katrina from Poland and a family from Australia. All these folks helped me out from time to time with my girls. I wondered if Sherri and Stephanie would ever again be satisfied with a regular baby-sitter after experiencing this ambience of international sitters.

Celebrating the New Year of 1983 was easier and gentler than 1982. I went to a party at Carolyn's. It was good to be with friends and to discover that my grief was not as consuming as it had been the year before. A few days later Narcotics Anonymous held a convention in Virginia Beach. I attended some lectures, as well as the evening dance. People had come from all over the east coast. I had a great time, and I met some new people. One of them was Stan, who lived in Virginia Beach. As the night went on, the beginnings of a friendship emerged. He was not actually attending the conference; he was working for the hotel where it was held. He couldn't understand why these people drank so much coffee and neither could the rest of the hotel staff.

Stan and I dated for a short time following the convention. He was a nice, gentle man, who had recently been hurt by a girl he loved. His girlfriend had been into witchcraft and demons, and she had told him that he was a demon. This comment had hurt him and then it festered. He knew nothing of these things and wondered if she were right. His injured self-concept and willingness to discuss his pain opened my heart to him. I didn't fall in love with Stan, but I found it easy to be with him and safe. He listened to my pain, and he thought I was an attractive woman despite my mangled leg. As our friendship expanded, I told him about my own recovery, and he confessed his concerns about his own chemical use.

Relationships were helping me to open up and heal. So did new understandings that came from unusual sources: psychics. Because the A.R.E. was based on Edgar Cayce's psychic readings, often psychics from far and wide were attracted to the area. It was a good place for them to study and meet like-minded people. I had many readings and some in particular were very helpful. One indicated to me that telling my children stories at night would assist them in going to sleep with pleasant thoughts on their minds. The psychic said that my voice was soothing to them, and it would diminish their nightmares.

Ever since Steve's death, both children suffered with nightmares. A typical evening involved two or three nightmares between them. It had been happening for so long, I had gotten used to the process of getting up several times during the night. But clearly something needed to change, so I decided to give the psychic's suggestions a try.

The stories I created as I sat with my children were so good that I decided to tape record them as I told them. When I got tired of telling new stories, I let the girls listen to the tapes I had made of previous ones. Eventually the stories helped, but it was another year before the nightmares completely stopped. The time it took was symbolic of the total healing process that all three of us were going through. There were no quick-fix techniques. Patience and persistence were vital.

When the new year began, Kurt started coming to my house. After our brief encounter early in December, he had left town. When he returned to Virginia Beach, he arrived at my door to visit. When I saw him, my feelings must have been like Mary-Jo's when I came knocking at the door of her mission. Mary-Jo had said

I was everything she didn't need: a pretty, young woman, who was needy and vulnerable. Kurt was everything I didn't need: newly sober, a sailor in transition, young, and good-looking. He went right for my Achilles heel and sparked a fun relationship with my girls. He genuinely enjoyed them, and they enjoyed him. It didn't take me long to fall into his arms and surrender all my good sense. As my heart opened up to him, it felt as if it were tearing. It was physically painful for me to love again. I still felt raw inside. I think Kurt came into my life to help me keep my heart open.

He offered me things I treasured. He was honest and liked to talk things out. He had respect for what I had accomplished in my life, and he loved my girls. His interests were similar to mine, and he was intellectually stimulating.

It was a time of transition in his life. He was leaving the Navy and deciding what he wanted to do with the rest of his life. In February, when his apartment lease ended, I invited him to stay at my house, utilizing the bedroom recently vacated by my English boarder, Virginia, who was now heading home.

In March, Kurt made it clear that he was going home to go back to school. It was inconceivable to me that he would leave. As the time grew closer, he withdrew from our relationship emotionally. Finally the day came when he left. I was devastated and so were the girls. Our house started to feel unbearably dark, dirty, and depressing. I felt as if I were suffocating, and I wondered how I had lived there so long. We found another house on the other side of the beach, and we moved May 1.

This house was a two-story A-frame with vaulted ceilings. It felt spacious and new. The girls loved it, although we were now ten blocks from the beach. I started seriously to consider not going back to Minnesota. When we moved into the house, I had asked Pat to drive down with my furniture. He arrived on schedule and helped us unpack and get settled. It was sad to see him leave; he had been there for me since the day of Steve's accident when I had asked him to come to the hospital. He had taught me to share and trust. He showed me that people could be there and support me if I let them. His help had been available for me when I was most in need. As it turned out, I saw Pat only one more time. His visit to Virginia Beach was really the last time we had the chance to enjoy the friendship we had developed.

It felt good to have my own furniture back with me again. Our neighbors were friendly, and we felt comfortable in our new home. What's more, I found that I could sleep in a bedroom again.

Nancy and I had worked continuously on my leg for a year. I was ready to stop our treatments. We had accomplished many of our goals. My ankle and knee swelled less frequently and to a much lesser degree. My thigh had strengthened considerably, and I rarely experienced pain. My calf still appeared flat, but I assumed that would be its permanent condition. The color of my leg was healthy, the result of improved circulation and increased time in the sun. Nancy presented our data to a Holistic Nursing Conference. I came along and allowed the nurses to see firsthand how healthy my leg looked. They were impressed, and it seemed to be the perfect conclusion to our work together.

[27]

Occasionally I contacted my lawyer, David, to find out what was happening with the lawsuit. During one of these phone calls, we discussed what he thought was a reasonable settlement. He told me I could expect one to two million dollars. On June 7 he called to tell me that an offer had been made for $150,000. I asked if this was a joke. The two amounts weren't even close. I knew $50,000 would go to David and another $20,000 for hospital bills. That meant about $80,000 for my girls and me. I asked if we were supposed to make a counteroffer now. He told me, "Gayle, this is not TV. They make an offer, and you either take it or leave it."

I asked why they would make such a low offer. He replied that sometimes people get tired of the litigation and just want out. It's a weeding-out process. He advised me not to accept the offer because we had such a good case. I followed his advice.

The girls and I flew to Minneapolis to join David and Steve's sister Linda. Then we all flew out to South Dakota for the jury trial on June 14. At the airport I met

Mallard. He also had retained David to represent him in a similar lawsuit from his own accident the same night as Steve's. It was the first time I knew that there were two lawsuits involved.

Praise the Lord that Linda was there! Court was a nightmare. The opposing attorney presented to the jury that Steve was a cocaine biker from the city who would rather buy drugs than shoes for his children. He pictured me as the bereaved widow who was looking to have South Dakota's tax dollars support me in a way that Steve never did.

I was in shock that slanderous statements could be made about Steve and me in a courtroom. I was amazed that a trial could revolve around the mythical portraits painted by a lawyer rather than around the issues of the case. After two grueling weeks, we received a second offer for settlement. I asked David if they had increased the offer and he responded, "Gayle, they are not going to increase their offer."

I told David I was confused and felt that the trial wasn't going well. He said he thought things were going really well, and the second offer showed that the opponents were getting nervous. He recommended that I turn the offer down, which I did. The next day the jury deliberated for twenty minutes and found for South Dakota. We left without a dime and many bills.

I flew back to Virginia feeling deeply our defeat. It was over, and I was glad—a nightmare I never wanted to repeat. A cloud of mistrust had formed concerning our judicial system. Doubts about the competency of my lawyer filled my mind. A feeling of powerlessness consumed me. I withdrew to re-evaluate my life and the direction I wanted to go.

I realized that I wanted to go home—back to Minnesota, back to my family and friends. It was so clear now. My life was there. My brief work experience in Virginia had shown me that if I ever wanted to have a challenging position I would need more schooling. I had recently finished my certificate training program that required bimonthly trips back to the University of Minnesota. But I could see that I needed a lot more education and decided to go back to college and get my B.A.

My life was ready to begin again. My healing was solidly under way—from the inside issues of self-love and forgiveness to the outside matter of rebuilding my leg. In fact, I now felt that I had successfully restored my leg to a healthy state. My grief had healed enough for me to feel motivated to design a new life for myself. The children had healed and had become strong enough to return to a traditional school system. I felt as if I could breathe again.

The night before we left, Stan, whom I had met at the Narcotics Anonymous conference, knocked on my door. I was surprised to see him. It had been months. He heard I had moved to the other side of the beach and had been searching for me ever since. He told me he wanted what I had—sobriety—and he wanted to know how to get it. I gave him phone numbers of people who would show him the way. Stan's visit was a great good-bye gift from the Virginia Beach community.

Steve came to me in a dream on my last night there. When I saw him, he said, "I love you."

I looked into his brown eyes and replied, "I love you, too."

Then he said, "I stayed away so you could have your own life. I'm glad you know that Virginia Beach isn't where you'll find happiness. I'm glad you're moving home."

[Epilogue]

This has been the story of four years in my incredible healing journey. As I suffered loss after loss, something deep within me began to emerge. At first a traumatic accident took me away from my children and the life that I knew. It made me focus in on healing my body. Then I had a brief love affair that initiated a greater love affair with my husband. We healed much of the strife that was between us. Next, the loss of my husband left an open wound in my heart and the hearts of my daughters. I left everything I knew to go in search of healing—for my heart, my leg, and my children.

When Steve died, I asked God if the love that I sought so desperately from Steve would be provided in a form that I could touch and smell. The answer has been yes, though not quite the way I might have expected. It has been love presented to me in as many creative forms as I could experience it: people, dreams, healing, houses, opportunities, and insights. This love has been a constant in my ever-changing world. The universe, the Lord, the Source, has kept providing me with everything I have needed to heal—to become truly whole.

After my year in Virginia Beach, my new life unfolded in Minnesota. I completed my educational goals by attaining a master's degree in vocational rehabilitation. I have remembered the promise I made with God in 1979. I wanted a total healing in ten years and in return I would tell my story and devote my life to service. It's been an incredibly full ten years!

During this time I've worked on coming to terms with the way my leg looks and testing its potential. I've found that I'm comfortable with a two-mile walk, but I've done up to eleven miles. On a good day I'm in awe of the miracle, and on a bad day I'm still sensitive to stares. But most often my leg is to me just another body part, only needing attention on rare occasions.

In 1987 I had some trouble with my left knee. I went to see an orthopedist to get his opinion on the cause of the pain I was experiencing. We had never before met, and when he looked at the X-rays and at my leg, he was astonished that I was walking so well. He asked me to walk back and forth in front of him. Then he asked how was I able to walk as well as I did. I told him I could do it this well because I didn't know I couldn't. In response to my inquiry he informed me that I had arthritis in my knee. Later, a friend gave me a spiritual healing which relieved the pain. Since then, the only indications of arthritis are cracking sounds when I bend deeply.

In March of 1992, shortly after I signed the contract to publish this book, I went back to Dr. Gustillo about a small wound on the front of my left leg that wasn't healing. The skin in this area, usually red, consisted of scar tissue and skin grafts. Its irregular surface was made up of bumps and pits. In the past, I had consistently injured this spot. I had no feeling there, so I found this condition irritating but not painful.

Dr. Gustillo hadn't seen my leg in many years. He suggested that I have another surgery to reconstruct this area. He was concerned that there was inadequate blood supply at this site and that these skin cells had been damaged much too often to assure prolonged healthy tissue.

It was a shock to think about going back into surgery. As I prepared myself to revisit old memories, I became conscious of the terror stored in my body. This terror was so consuming that I found it difficult to utilize the tools that I had gained these past thirteen years: trust in divine order, prayer, meditation, and affirmations. I had to lean on those around me to help me through this opportunity.

My name went on several prayer lists, and I reconnected with Beth for absentee healings. Working with her revived the positive, nurturing feelings we had previously established. I also went to a hypnotherapist to assist me in speaking to my body, preparing it for the changes the surgeon would make. My friends allowed me to ventilate my fears with them, escorted me to doctor appointments, and supported me throughout this experience.

The day of my surgery—April 20, 1992—my children took me to the hospital and stayed by my side, seeing for the first time what had taken their mother away from them so many years ago. The anesthesiologist spoke with me about alternative drugs for my surgery that might not make me feel so sick afterward. The I.V. was inserted on the first try, and my request to avoid the backs of my hands was respected.

Following surgery, I was sick for one day. I felt as if I had been poisoned, and it took about twenty-four hours for my body to rid itself of these medications. The anesthesiologist told me that they had done their best, but that some people still react the way I did. Fortunately, my body bounced back quickly after the anesthesia cleared out. I found no need for pain medication, so my I.V. was disconnected the day after my surgery. Another positive element of this period of time was my father's presence. He visited me daily and distracted me with interesting tales from his life. I appreciated very much his time with me.

The operation had been done in two steps: reconstructive surgery followed by a skin graft. When I woke from surgery, my leg was pain-free, and the only way I could find the donor site was to see the bandage. I learned that the surgeon had taken a piece of skin from the back and side of my left leg and moved it around to the front. One end of the skin actually remained attached to its original spot on the side of my leg. With this technique, a thick chunk of skin was moved, including the vascular tissue under it. This reconstructive surgery was quite different from my previous grafts, in which only a thin layer of skin was moved.

This thin-layer approach was the second step of the new surgery, since an open, wedge-shaped area was created on the back of my leg by the first step. To cover it, some skin was grafted from my thigh down to this spot. Consequently, I had a bandage over this area on my thigh. But I was relieved to learn that modern medicine had devised a new bandage that covered the donor site and allowed it to heal in a painless fashion. I have agonizing memories of my bandages being torn off the donor site after my previous skin-graft surgery. But this new bandage didn't stick to the wound, and the bandage changes on my thigh were painless.

My one complaint in the days following surgery was a stiff neck. I was thinking how a massage might be helpful when my friend Betsy came to visit. Coincidentally, she's a massage therapist. Her skilled hands relieved my discomfort for a few hours. But as the second night approached, my stiff neck returned. It seemed to be getting worse. The pain spread down my shoulders, into my back, and up into the right side of my face.

After a painful night, I asked the nurse on duty for a recommendation to ease my neck pain. She responded,

"The lady next door to you woke up with a stiff neck, too, and she called a chiropractor to help her."

"What a wonderful idea!" I thought, surprised to receive such a suggestion from a nurse in an orthopedic ward. I called my chiropractor friend Karen and asked if she could come to the hospital to adjust me. She told me that she was already planning to visit me that day and would be glad to accommodate me.

Karen's adjustment relieved the pain until evening. On this third night, I again had intense pain in my neck, shoulder, back, jaw, and clavicle. At this point I realized that some emotional pain was trapped in my body, since the treatments I had been receiving should have cleared up these problems by now. In the morning I called a healer, Claire, who I knew lived nearby. I asked if she had time to give me a hands-on healing. She said, "I'm so glad you called. I just happened to have some spare time today."

During the hands-on healing, I became conscious of my own sadness surrounding the impact of my accident. In my mind I revisited the day of the accident and felt the immensity of this life event. But instead of re-encountering exact details, I more or less reviewed the experience as a whole. Through Claire's healing gift and my own inner experience, I released the energy trapped in my body, and the pain left. After this session with Claire ended, what remained was a deep sense of completion and wholeness.

Three days after the surgery, when the doctors removed the bandages from my leg, it was clear the operation had been a success. Then I realized I had been given another gift. The front of my leg appeared more normal. The skin the surgeon had moved there had feeling in it. It was smooth, looked full, and had a healthy skin tone. What's more, all of the skin grafted onto the back of my leg had adhered.

I believe that this part of my life's journey has come to an end. No doubt, other adventurous challenges lie ahead. But in this space between adventures, I feel a deep sense of hope, joy, and expectation. In my heart I feel safe, blessed, and at peace. Thank You, Father.

What Is A.R.E.®?

The Association for Research and Enlightenment, Inc. (A.R.E.), is the international headquarters for the work of Edgar Cayce (1877-1945), who is considered the best-documented psychic of the twentieth century. Founded in 1931, the A.R.E. consists of a community of people from all walks of life and spiritual traditions, who have found meaningful and life-transformative insights from the readings of Edgar Cayce.

Although A.R.E. headquarters is located in Virginia Beach, Virginia—where visitors are always welcome—the A.R.E. community is a global network of individuals who offer conferences, educational activities, and fellowship around the world. People of every age are invited to participate in programs that focus on such topics as holistic health, dreams, reincarnation, ESP, the power of the mind, meditation, and personal spirituality.

In addition to study groups and various activities, the A.R.E. offers membership benefits and services, a bimonthly magazine, a newsletter, extracts from the Cayce readings, conferences, international tours, a massage school curriculum, an impressive volunteer network, a retreat-type camp for children and adults, and A.R.E. contacts around the world. A.R.E. also maintains an affiliation with Atlantic University, which offers a master's degree program in Transpersonal Studies.

For additional information about A.R.E. activities hosted near you, please contact:

A.R.E.
67th St. and Atlantic Ave.
P.O. Box 595
Virginia Beach, VA 23451-0595
(804) 428-3588

A.R.E. Press

A.R.E. Press is a publisher and distributor of books, audiotapes, and videos that offer guidance for a more fulfilling life. Our products are based on, or are compatible with, the concepts in the psychic readings of Edgar Cayce.

We especially seek to create products which carry forward the inspirational story of individuals who have made practical application of the Cayce legacy.

For a free catalog, please write to A.R.E. Press at the address below or call toll free 1-800-723-1112. For any other information, please call 804-428-3588, extension 220.

A.R.E. Press
Sixty-Eighth & Atlantic Avenue
P.O. Box 656
Virginia Beach, VA 23451-0656